MOVIES AND TV

THE NEW YORK PUBLIC LIBRARY

BOOK OF ANSWERS

MELINDA COREY AND GEORGE OCHOA

A Stonesong Press Book
A Fireside Book
Published by Simon & Schuster
New York ◆ London ◆ Toronto ◆ Sydney ◆ Tokyo ◆ Singapore

♦ ♦ ♦

To the movie-loving friends
of our youth:
Roy
— G.O
Sue
— M.C.

FIRESIDE
Simon & Schuster Building
Rockefeller Center
1230 Avenue of the Americas
New York, New York 10020

Designed by Diane Stevenson/Snap-Haus Graphics
Manufactured in the United States of America

1   3   5   7   9   10   8   6   4   2

Library of Congress Cataloging in Publication Data is available
ISBN: 0-671-77538-3

TABLE OF CONTENTS

◆ ◆ ◆

MOVIES AND TV:
THE NEW YORK PUBLIC LIBRARY
BOOK OF ANSWERS

◆ ◆ ◆

INTRODUCTION

This is a sequel to *The Book of Answers*, a collection of over one thousand questions and answers inspired by the world-famous New York Public Library Telephone Reference Service (Tel Ref). The aim for any sequel is to be vastly different from and yet in the same spirit as its original. This is what we have tried to do with *Movies and TV: The New York Public Library Book of Answers*.

In *The Book of Answers*, we addressed questions in twenty-seven different subject areas, from American History to Who Was Who, to provide a flavor for the breadth of information handled by Tel Ref. For sequels to *The Book of Answers*, we decided instead to focus on the depth of information that the New York Public Library (NYPL) can provide.

Why choose movies and television for the first sequel? There are several reasons.

First, people like movies and television shows. They know them. They are part of our history. People remember that first sight of Bogart in a trenchcoat or Liz Taylor in a slip, the debates about how the Red Sea was parted, the times when their father *was* Archie Bunker. This common knowledge makes movies and TV shows rich sources for friendly arguments and office bets, and as a result, they are among Tel Ref's most popular subjects. (These subjects also happen to be broad enough to sustain a book. Presidents Who Have Served in the Armed Forces is a popular Tel Ref topic, but a book about it might get tedious after a few pages.)

Second, despite the many reference books on the subjects, there are still questions that most TV and movie books leave unanswered. What was the last picture show in *The Last Picture Show*? Where was the stagecoach headed in *Stagecoach*? Who played Gentle Ben?

The third reason is simpler: the authors like this subject area. Long before we became coauthors (or spouses), our first date was a movie, a double bill of Anthony Mann's *The Far Country* and Wim Wenders's *Kings of the Road*. In talking about movies and TV, we have the same arguments and lapses of memory as our readers. What was the name of the dinosaur bone in *Bringing Up Baby*? What did Gomer Pyle do before he entered the Marines? As researchers, we have found the best way to find the book we need is sometimes to write it.

The first *Book of Answers* contains only questions that could be answered by the New York Public Library's general reference service. This book and those that follow will go deeper, drawing on the resources of the entire New York Public Library system. Some of the questions in this book are the kind that the general reference service would refer to the NYPL Arts Division. Some would only be answered by your sitting with the books themselves. In short, this book may save you and the librarians a lot of work.

To make *Movies and TV: The New York Public Library Book of Answers* easy to use, we have separated the book into three parts: "Movies," "Television," and "Movies and Television." "Movies" contains sections like Westerns; Remakes and Sequels; and Oscars and Other Awards. "Television" contains Situation Comedies; Soap Operas and Game Shows; and Commercials. "Movies and Television" covers the connections between the two media—in actors, subject matter, and content. (What was the first movie based on a TV series? What movie about a genie featured Barbara Eden?) Also included in this part of the book are sections carried over from the first *Book of Answers,* including Omnibus (in how many movies did Elvis die?); the Question and Answer Hall of Fame (who played Carlton the Doorman?); and Trick Questions and Popular Delusions (who sang for Lauren Bacall in *To Have and Have Not?*).

Although *Movies and TV: The New York Public Library Book of Answers* can be neither as comprehensive nor as sober as an encyclopedia, it is entirely factual and provides an impressionistic history of each form. Each section of the book moves in chronological order—from Chaplin to Selznick to Schwarzenegger in "Movies"; from Milton Berle to Mary Tyler Moore to Ted Turner in "Television."

As with its predecessor, *Movies and TV: The New York Public Library Book of Answers* leaves some mysteries unsolved. (What attracted Julia Roberts to Kiefer Sutherland? How could Ben Cartwright have three sons who did not resemble him or one another?) But a wide variety of entertainment answers are provided—like the names of Arnold Ziffel's parents and whether Krakatoa is east of Java. These are the facts; the arguments about them are left to you.

—Melinda Corey and George Ochoa

PART·I
· MOVIES ·

ACTION AND ADVENTURE

♦ ♦ ♦

What was "Little Caesar" 's real name?
Caesar Enrico Bandello, played by Edward G. Robinson in the 1930 film.

What was the first Fu Manchu movie made as a sound feature?
The Mysterious Dr. Fu Manchu (1929), starring Warner Oland.

In how many swashbucklers did Errol Flynn and Basil Rathbone cross swords?
Two—*Captain Blood* (1935) and *The Adventures of Robin Hood* (1938). The two also acted together in *The Dawn Patrol* (1938).

What historical event does *Thirty Seconds Over Tokyo* (1944) commemorate?

It depicts the first American air raid on Japan, staged in 1942 by Lt. Colonel Jimmy Doolittle (played by Spencer Tracy). The movie was based on the book of the same name by Ted Lawrence, a pilot on the raid (Van Johnson). The air strike was important in lifting American morale early in World War II.

Who directed *Around the World in 80 Days* (1956)?
Michael Anderson. Mike Todd produced.

> *Who wrote the score?*
> Victor Young. The score won an Oscar.

> *Who wrote the screenplay?*
> S. J. Perelman. John Farrow and James Poe were uncredited contributors.

Where was gladiator-film star Steve Reeves born?
In Glasgow, Montana, in 1926. The bodybuilding champion became famous in Italian mythological epics beginning with *Hercules* (aka *Le Fatiche di Ercole*) in 1957.

John Ford's *The Wings of Eagles* (1957) is based on the life of what famous flyer?
World War I aviator Frank "Spig" Wead, who after a debilitating accident, became a screenwriter. The screenplays he wrote included *Air Mail* (1932), *The Citadel* (1938), and *They Were Expendable* (1945).

In what movie did Vincent Gardenia play gangster "Dutch" Schultz?
Mad Dog Coll (1961).

What does *hatari* mean?
It is Swahili for "danger." *Hatari!* was a 1962 film starring John Wayne and Elsa Martinelli.

What is the name of Dr. No's island in *Dr. No* (1962)?
Crab Key.

What does "SPECTRE" in the James Bond films stand for?
"Special Executive for Counterintelligence, Terrorism, Revenge, and Extortion."

Who has played Miss Moneypenny in most of the James Bond films?
Lois Maxwell.

> *Who has played M?*
> Bernard Lee until his death in 1979; Robert Brown since then.

> *Who has played Q?*
> Desmond Llewelyn.

Whom did private eye Matt Helm work for?
Played by Dean Martin, he was a secret service agent for ICE (Organization for Intelligence and Counter-Espionage). The four Matt Helm movies were: *The Silencers* (1966), *Murderer's Row* (1966), *The Ambassadors* (1967), and *The Wrecking Crew* (1969). The character is taken from a series of novels by Donald Hamilton.

Who was Shaft in the movie of the same name. (1971)?
John Shaft, "the black private dick that's a sex machine to all the chicks," was played by Richard Roundtree. The Oscar-winning "Theme from *Shaft*" was by Isaac Hayes.

Who was the inspiration for Jimmy "Popeye" Doyle in *The French Connection* (1971)?
New York City policeman Eddie Egan.

Why did "Dirty Harry" say he was called "dirty"?
Because he does "every dirty job that comes along." Clint Eastwood played Harry Callahan.

How many "Dirty Harry" movies have been made?
Five: *Dirty Harry* (1971), *Magnum Force* (1973), *The Enforcer* (1976), *Sudden Impact* (1983), and *The Dead Pool* (1988).

What was the name of the Russian boxer faced by Rocky Balboa (Sylvester Stallone) in *Rocky IV* (1985)?
Drago (Dolph Lundgren).

How many times has the story of Baron Munchausen been filmed?
Three, with these actors starring as the Baron:

Baron Müenchhausen (1943, Germany)—Hans Albers
The Fabulous Baron Munchausen (1961, Czechoslova-
 kia)—Milos Kopecky

The Adventures of Baron Munchausen (1989)—John Neville

What actors preceded Warren Beatty in the role of *Dick Tracy* (1990)?
Ralph Byrd played the part in the Republic (and later RKO) series beginning with *Dick Tracy* (1937). Morgan Conway played the police detective in two RKO films, beginning with *Dick Tracy* (1945).

Who played Robin Hood's sidekick Little John in *The Adventures of Robin Hood* (1938)?
Alan Hale, alongside Errol Flynn as Robin.

> *Who played the part in* Robin and Marian *(1976)?*
> Nicol Williamson, alongside Sean Connery.

> *In* Robin Hood: Prince of Thieves *(1991)?*
> Nick Brimble, alongside Kevin Costner.

What is the time setting of *Raiders of the Lost Ark* (1981)?
1936.

> *What about* Indiana Jones and the Temple of Doom *(1984)?*
> 1935.

> Indiana Jones and the Last Crusade *(1989)?*
> It opens in 1912, then shifts to 1938.

ANIMALS AND CHILDREN
♦ ♦ ♦

What was the first Mickey Mouse cartoon?

The first one produced was *Plane Crazy* (1928). The second was *Gallopin' Gaucho* (1928). The third was *Steamboat Willie* (1928), the first Mickey Mouse sound cartoon.

Who invented "Felix the Cat"?

An artist named Otto Messmer who worked for silent cartoon animator Pat Sullivan. Messmer developed Felix for Paramount's *Screen Magazine* in 1919. Paramount producer John King gave Felix his name. The first Felix cartoon in 1919 was called *Feline Follies;* the second was called *Musical Mews.*

How old was Judy Garland when she made *The Wizard of Oz* (1939)?

Sixteen.

What was Elizabeth Taylor's screen debut?
There's One Born Every Minute in 1942. Taylor was nine at the time.

When did the "Dead End Kids" become the "East Side Kids"?
In 1940, when producer Sam Katzman brought some of the kids to Monogram Pictures. The kids (who eventually included Leo Gorcey, Huntz Hall, Bobby Jordan, Billy Halop, and others) had started out as the "Dead End Kids" in *Dead End* (1937, Samuel Goldwyn). They had gone on to work for Warner Brothers and Universal. Their first Monogram film was *East Side Kids* (1940).

> *When did they become the "Bowery Boys"?*
> In 1946, with *In Fast Company,* also at Monogram. There were a total of seventy "East Side" and "Bowery Boys" films.

What was the name of Gene Autry's horse?
Champion, the Wonder Horse.

What ever happened to Bonzo of *Bedtime for Bonzo* (1951)?
The chimp died in a trailer fire in the early 1950s, along with his four stand-ins, on the day he was scheduled to help present the first Patsy Awards for animal achievement.

When was the Warner Brothers cartoon short *Duck Dodgers in the 24½ Century* released?

July 25, 1953. Chuck Jones directed; Daffy Duck and Porky Pig starred.

Who played the infant Moses in *The Ten Commandments* (1956)?
Charlton Heston's son, Fraser.

What ever happened to Fraser Heston?
Fraser Clarke Heston went on to write the screenplay for *The Mountain Men* (1980), a film starring his father. He also wrote and produced *Mother Lode* (1982), again starring his father. Charlton Heston also codirected the latter film, with Joe Canutt, son of Western actor Yakima Canutt.

Who played Flipper in *Flipper* (1963)?
Mitzi. Susie played the dolphin in the sequel, *Flipper's New Adventure* (1964), and in the TV series "Flipper" (NBC, 1964–68).

Who wrote the book on which *Chitty Chitty Bang Bang* (1968) is based?
James Bond creator Ian Fleming.

Who did the voice of the dog in *A Boy and His Dog* (1975)?
Tim McIntire gave his voice to the telepathic dog Blood in this post-apocalyptic science fiction movie. Blood himself was played by Tiger of TV's "The Brady Bunch" (ABC, 1969–74).

Which Clint Eastwood movies featured an orangutan?
Every Which Way But Loose (1978) and *Any Which Way You Can* (1980). The orangutan's name was Clyde.

What actress grew up into Whoopi Goldberg in *The Color Purple* (1985)?
Desreta Jackson, who played Celie as a child.

Where is Rin Tin Tin buried?
The canine silent movie star is buried under a black onyx tombstone inscribed "The Greatest Cinema Star" in Cimetière du Chiens in Paris, France.

BOOKS INTO FILM

♦ ♦ ♦

Who played Ahab in the original film version of *Moby Dick* **(1930)?**
John Barrymore.

> *Who played Ishmael?*
> No one. The character was cut out of the screenplay, which differed heavily from Herman Melville's novel.

Who plays Percy Shelley and Lord Byron in *The Bride of Frankenstein* **(1935)?**
In the prologue that frames the story, Douglas Walton plays Shelley and Gavin Gordon plays Lord Byron. Elsa Lanchester plays Mary Shelley (author of the novel *Frankenstein*), as well as the monster's bride.

What Alfred Hitchcock movie is based on a Joseph Conrad novel?

24

Sabotage (1936, UK; released in the U.S. as *A Woman Alone*). It was based on Conrad's *The Secret Agent*. It is not to be confused with Hitchcock's *The Secret Agent,* released earlier that year and based on Somerset Maugham's novel *Ashenden.*

Who wrote the screenplay for the original film version of *Pygmalion* (1938)?
The play's author, George Bernard Shaw, who won an Oscar for his adaptation.

Whom did author Margaret Mitchell suggest to MGM to play Rhett Butler in *Gone With the Wind* (1939)?
Groucho Marx, but only in jest.

On what book is *The Heiress* (1949) based?
Washington Square, by Henry James.

On what book was *A Place in the Sun* (1951) based?
An American Tragedy, by Theodore Dreiser.

Who wrote *Shane*, the book on which the 1953 movie is based?
Jack Schaefer.

Who wrote *A Summer Place*, the book on which the 1959 movie is based?
Sloan Wilson, author of *The Man in the Gray Flannel Suit.*

Who played Raskolnikov in *Crime and Punishment USA* (1959)?
George Hamilton played Robert Cole, a character based on Raskolnikov, in this strange version of Feodor Dostoevsky's *Crime and Punishment* set in Santa Monica, California. It was Hamilton's screen debut.

What was the first in the series of films produced by Roger Corman and American International Pictures (AIP) that were "inspired" by the works of Edgar Allan Poe?
House of Usher (1960; aka *The Fall of the House of Usher*). Like most of the films in the series—which also included *The Masque of the Red Death* (1964) and *The Pit and the Pendulum* (1961)—it starred Vincent Price.

Who wrote the short story on which Alfred Hitchcock's *The Birds* (1963) is based?
Daphne du Maurier.

On what work was *Dr. Strangelove* (1964) based?
A novel, *Red Alert*, by Peter George.

Who wrote *Summer of '42*, the book on which the 1971 movie is based?
Herman Raucher.

How many of his own novels has William Goldman adapted for the screen?
Four: *Marathon Man* (1976), *Magic* (1978), *Heat* (1987), and *The Princess Bride* (1987).

Was there ever a movie adaptation of Aldous Huxley's *Brave New World*?
There was never a theatrical movie version, but there was a 1980 TV movie starring Keir Dullea, Bud Cort, Julie Cobb, and Ron O'Neal.

What Stephen King work is the basis for *Stand by Me* (1986)?
The Body, a novella.

COMEDY

When was the first movie pie fight?

It was in 1913, for a Keystone Studio comedy. Mabel Normand tossed a workman's lemon meringue pie at Ben Turpin to get him to laugh. He did; Mack Sennett saw it and the pie scene became a favorite bit in Keystone Kop comedies—and in many other comedies as well.

Who was the "King of Daredevil Comedy"?

Harold Lloyd, whose best-known movie is *Safety Last* (1923).

What was the feature film debut of radio's "Amos 'n' Andy"?

Check and Double Check (1930) was the first film to star Freeman F. Gosden as Amos and Charles V. Correll as

Andy. The two white actors played the roles in black-face.

Who were the "Three Stooges"?
Making their debut in *Soup to Nuts* (1930), they were Moe Howard, Larry Fine, and a string of actors in the third role: Shemp Howard, Jerry "Curly" Howard, Joe Besser, and Joe De Rita.

Which Marx Brothers movie featured Groucho singing "Hooray for Captain Spaulding"?
Animal Crackers (1930). Groucho's character was Captain Jeffrey Spaulding, the African explorer.

What was Zeppo's last film with the Marx Brothers?
Duck Soup (1933).

What were the names of the mythical countries in *Duck Soup* (1933)?
Freedonia and Sylvania.

> *What was the mythical country in* Million Dollar Legs *(1932)?*
> Klopstokia.

> *What was the mythical country in* The Mouse That Roared *(1959)?*
> The Duchy of Grand Fenwick.

To whom did the million-dollar legs belong in the 1939 movie *Million Dollar Legs*?

To a racehorse by the same name. Betty Grable's legs and the rest of the actress appeared in the movie too.

Where was the dinner at eight held in *Dinner at Eight* (1933)?
At the Park Avenue home of Mr. and Mrs. Oliver Jordan.

> *Who were supposed to be the guests of honor?*
> Lord and Lady Ferncliffe. They never showed.

How many times did Ralph Bellamy play the "other man" with whom Cary Grant had to compete for the heroine's affections?
Twice—in *The Awful Truth* (1937), where Irene Dunne was the woman; and in *His Girl Friday* (1940), where Rosalind Russell was the woman.

What was the name of the dinosaur bone lost by David Huxley (Cary Grant) in *Bringing Up Baby* (1938)?
An intercostal clavicle.

What was the award-winning coffee slogan devised by Dick Powell in Preston Sturges's *Christmas in July* (1940)?
"If you can't sleep at night, it isn't the coffee—it's the bunk."

For what magazine did Macauley Connor work in *The Philadelphia Story* (1940)?
Spy magazine.

What was the name of director John L. Sullivan's (Joel McCrea's) "serious" film that he wanted to research in *Sullivan's Travels* (1941)?

Oh Brother, Where Art Thou? was the film in planning that set him on the road. He had become famous doing popular movies like *Hey Hey in the Hayloft* and *So Long, Sarong*.

How many of Bob Hope's movies have the word *favorite* in the title?

Three: *My Favorite Blonde* (1942), *My Favorite Brunette* (1947), and *My Favorite Spy* (1951).

In what film did Ava Gardner appear with the Bowery Boys?

Ghosts on the Loose (1943), which also starred Bela Lugosi, Leo Gorcey, and Huntz Hall. Gardner played Huntz Hall's sister.

What was the miracle in *Miracle of Morgan's Creek* (1944)?

It was the birth of sextuplets to Trudy Kockenlocker (Betty Hutton), a woman who got married and pregnant without remembering it after drinking too much at a World War II servicemen's dance.

What movie gave Ma and Pa Kettle their debut?

The Egg and I (1947), about a city woman (Claudette Colbert) who marries a chicken farmer (Fred MacMurray). Ma and Pa Kettle were supporting characters played by Marjorie Main and Percy Kilbride. They went on to star in the same roles in their own movie series.

How many movies did Boris Karloff make with Abbott and Costello?
Two: *Abbott and Costello Meet the Killer, Boris Karloff* (1949), and *Abbott and Costello Meet Dr. Jekyll and Mr. Hyde* (1953). Karloff did not appear in *Abbott and Costello Meet Frankenstein* (1948), where Glenn Strange played the Frankenstein monster.

How many parts does Alec Guinness play in *Kind Hearts and Coronets* (1949)?
He plays all of the eight members of an aristocratic family killed off in this dark comedy.

How tall was Harvey the Rabbit?
Playwright Mary Chase placed Harvey, the invisible rabbit companion of Elwood P. Dowd, at six feet, one and a half inches tall. Elwood P. Dowd was played by James Stewart in the movie version of *Harvey* (1950).

> *How tall is James Stewart?*
> Six feet, three and a half inches tall.

What was the name of the ship in *Mister Roberts* (1955)?
The USS *Reluctant.*

What was the last movie Jerry Lewis and Dean Martin made together?

It was *Hollywood or Bust* (1956). It ended a successful string of seventeen releases, beginning in 1949 with *My Friend Irma.*

In *Will Success Spoil Rock Hunter* (1957), what product brought adman Rock Hunter (Tony Randall) to sudden fame?
Stay-Put Lipstick, which was endorsed by sex symbol Rita Marlowe (Jayne Mansfield).

How many "Carry On" films were produced in Great Britain?
Twenty-nine, beginning with *Carry On Sergeant* (1958), and ending with *Carry On Emmanuelle* (1978).

Who moved like "Jell-O on springs" and in what movie?
According to Jerry/Daphne (Jack Lemmon), it was Marilyn Monroe as Sugar, in *Some Like It Hot* (1959).

Who starred in the 1939 *Some Like It Hot*?
Bob Hope and Una Merkel.

In *The Apartment* (1960), what does the "C. C." in C. C. Baxter stand for?
Calvin Clifford. The character was played by Jack Lemmon.

What were the names of the dual characters played by Jerry Lewis in *The Nutty Professor* (1963)?

Professor Julius Ferris Kelp was the nutty professor. Buddy Love was his suave, lounge-singing alter ego.

Who was Robin in *Robin and the Seven Hoods* (1964)?
Robbo, the character "inspired" by Robin Hood, was played by Frank Sinatra. Among the hoods were Dean Martin as Little John and Sammy Davis, Jr., as Will.

What Japanese spy film did Woody Allen dub with his own comic dialogue in *What's Up, Tiger Lily?* (1966)?
Kagi No Kag (1964), or *Key of Keys,* directed by Senkichi Taniguchi.

In what company did Robert Morse rise to the top in *How to Succeed in Business Without Really Trying* (1967)?
Window washer Morse conquered the Worldwide Wicket Co., owned by Rudy Vallee.

What was the name of the Broadway play with which Zero Mostel and Gene Wilder tried to fleece their investors in *The Producers* (1968)?
Springtime for Hitler.

> *Who was the play's author?*
> Nazi refugee Franz Liebkind, played by Kenneth Mars.

Who has been killing spiders since he was thirty?
Alvy Singer (Woody Allen) in *Annie Hall* (1977).

In *Annie Hall,* what does Woody Allen claim is the only cultural advantage offered by Los Angeles?
You can make a right turn on a red light.

What campus was used as the location for *Animal House* (1978)?
The University of Oregon–Eugene.

What slogan was used to promote God (George Burns) in *Oh, God, Book II* (1980)?
"Think God."

Who provided the voice of the brain with which Steve Martin falls in love in *The Man With Two Brains* (1983)?
Sissy Spacek.

What was the name of the art gallery worker with the funny accent in *Beverly Hills Cop* (1984)?
Serge, played by Bronson Pinchot.

What are the names of the *Ghostbusters* (1984)?
Dr. Peter Venkman (Bill Murray), Dr. Raymond Stantz (Dan Aykroyd), Dr. Egon Spengler (Harold Ramis), and Winston Zeddemore (Ernie Hudson).

How many 1988 films featured the premise of body-switching between a young person and an older person?
Three: *18 Again, Vice Versa,* and *Like Father, Like Son.* A fourth, *Big,* dealt with a young person magically ma-

tured into an older one. The premise dates back to the 1947 *Vice Versa*, where a child (Anthony Newley) switched bodies with his father (Roger Livesey).

For how much a week did Richard Gere hire Julia Roberts in *Pretty Woman* (1990)?
Three thousand dollars a week—cash.

What is the name of the fictitious soap opera in *Soapdish* (1991)?
"The Sun Also Sets."

DIRECTORS
♦ ♦ ♦

What did the *"D. W."* in director D. W. Griffith's name stand for?
David Wark (1874–1948).

What part did future director John Ford play in *The Birth of a Nation* (1915)?
He played a Ku Klux Klan member.

What was director John Ford's (1895–1973) real name?
Sean Aloysius O'Feeney.

What incident as a child in a police station helped to shape Alfred Hitchcock's sensibilities?
His father punished him for a since-forgotten offense by sending him to the police station with a note. The chief

of police read it and locked Hitchcock up for five to ten minutes, saying, "This is what we do to naughty boys." Hitchcock was four or five years old at the time.

What was Fritz Lang's first American film? His last?
Born in Vienna in 1890, the director came to Hollywood in 1934. His first American film was *Fury* (1936), for MGM. His last was *Beyond a Reasonable Doubt* (1956), for RKO. After that, the director quit making films in the United States, fed up with the trials and tribulations of the studio system. He died in 1976.

Did Hitchcock ever direct a costume drama?
Yes, two—*Jamaica Inn* (1939), and *Under Capricorn* (1949), both set in the nineteenth century. Hitchcock once said he didn't like to direct historical movies because he couldn't "imagine anyone in a costume picture ever going to the bathroom."

Where does director Alfred Hitchcock appear in *Rebecca* (1940)?
He passes by a phone booth being used by George Sanders.

> *Where does he appear in* Lifeboat *(1944)?*
> He can be seen in a weight-reduction ad in a newspaper.

> *Where does he appear in* Rope *(1948)?*
> His outline appears on a neon sign.

What was Laurence Olivier's directorial debut?
Henry V (1945).

For how many years was Leni Riefenstahl imprisoned after World War II?
The German director spent four years in a French detention camp after World War II for her activities as a Nazi filmmaker. Her last film was *Tiefland,* completed in 1954.

How many movies did David Lean make?
Sixteen.

> *How many times did he win the Oscar for best director?*
> Twice—for *The Bridge on the River Kwai* (1957) and *Lawrence of Arabia* (1962).

Did Walter Matthau ever direct a movie?
Only one—*Gangster Story* (1959). He both directed and starred in it.

How many films did John Wayne direct?
Two. He directed *The Alamo* (1960) and codirected *The Green Berets* (1968) with Ray Kellogg and (uncredited) Mervyn LeRoy. Wayne also directed some scenes (uncredited) of *The Comancheros* (1961, directed by Michael Curtiz).

Who was the original director of *Cleopatra* (1963)?

Rouben Mamoulian. After he was fired, Alfred Hitchcock was offered the job, but refused. Joseph L. Mankiewicz took over.

Who directed *The Terror* (1963)?
Only Roger Corman was billed as director, but several uncredited "assistants" helped out: Francis Ford Coppola, Monte Hellman, Jack Hill, Dennis Jacob, and Jack Nicholson.

Who played Mary in Pier Paolo Pasolini's *The Gospel According to St. Matthew* (1966)?
The director's mother, Susanna Pasolini.

How many people directed *Casino Royale* (1967)?
Five: John Huston, Ken Hughes, Robert Parrish, Joe McGrath, and Val Guest.

What was Paul Newman's directorial debut?
Rachel, Rachel (1968), starring his wife, Joanne Woodward.

What was the name of director Jonathan Demme's women-in-prison movie?
Caged Heat (1974), a low-budget epic released by New World. Demme also wrote the screenplay.

What part does director Roman Polanski play in his film *Repulsion* (1965)?
A spoons player.

What part does he play in his film Chinatown *(1974)?*
The man with the knife who cuts Jack Nicholson's nostril.

What was the first movie Gene Wilder directed?
The Adventure of Sherlock Holmes' Smarter Brother (1975). He also wrote the screenplay and starred as Sigerson Holmes.

How many female directors have been nominated for an Academy Award?
One. Lina Wertmuller was nominated for *Seven Beauties* in 1976. She didn't win.

What part does Martin Scorsese play in *Taxi Driver* (1976)?
He is an irate passenger in Travis Bickle's (Robert De-Niro's) cab—irate because his wife is having an affair.

What was George Lucas's last film as a director?
Star Wars (1977).

What was Robert Redford's directorial debut?
Ordinary People (1980).

Who directed *Airplane!* (1980)? How were the directors related?
Jim Abrahams, David Zucker, and Jerry Zucker directed. David and Jerry are brothers.

What was the first movie directed by Steven Spielberg associate Frank Marshall?
Arachnophobia (1990).

What films has Kevin Costner made with director and friend Kevin Reynolds?
Fandango (1985)—Costner's first starring role—and *Robin Hood: Prince of Thieves* (1991). Reynolds also shot second-unit footage on *Dances With Wolves* (1990), directed by Costner.

In how many movies directed by Martin Scorsese has his mother, Catherine Scorsese, appeared?
Four: *Who's That Knocking at My Door?* (1968), *Mean Streets* (1973), *The King of Comedy* (1983), and *Goodfellas* (1990).

How long, on average, does one have to wait for a new Stanley Kubrick movie?
Lately, about five years. In Kubrick's early period, from *Fear and Desire* (1953) to *Dr. Strangelove, or How I Learned to Stop Worrying and Love the Bomb* (1964), an average of 1.8 years passed between release of Kubrick's films. From *Dr. Strangelove* to *Full Metal Jacket* (1987), the average has been 4.6 years.

DRAMA

♦ ♦ ♦

Which of the little women in *Little Women* (1933) did Katharine Hepburn play?
Jo March, the eldest.

Who first played Dr. Kildare?
Joel McCrea, in *Interns Can't Take Money* (1937).

In *Gone With the Wind* (1939), were the Atlanta Civil War scenes shot on location?
No. Atlanta was built on the MGM studio back lot. Many of the burning buildings were recycled from movies like *King Kong* (1933), *Little Lord Fauntleroy* (1936), and *The Garden of Allah* (1936).

Where and when did *Mr. Smith Goes to Washington* (1939) have its premiere?

On October 16, 1939, on "Mr. Smith Day" in Washington, D.C., at Constitution Hall. The film was at first poorly received by members of the Senate, who felt that the movie cast a negative light on democracy and on Washington, D.C.

What are the closing lines of *The Grapes of Wrath* (1940)?
Jane Darwell says, "Can't nobody wipe us out. Can't nobody lick us. We'll go on forever, Pa. We're the people."

Where is Xanadu, Charles Foster Kane's estate in *Citizen Kane* (1941)?
On the Gulf Coast of Florida. The estate of William Randolph Hearst, on whom Kane was based, is located in San Simeon, California.

What is the name of the newsreel that recaps Kane's life in *Citizen Kane*?
"News on the March."

What is the name of Kane's first newspaper in *Citizen Kane*?
The New York Daily Inquirer.

Were "letters of transit" issued in World War II-era Casablanca?
No. "Letters of transit," authorizing people to travel without question, were a fiction used in the movie *Casablanca* (1942).

What was the name of the bartender in Rick's Cafe Americain in *Casablanca*?
Sascha (Leonid Kinskey).

How did "Mildred Pierce" build her fortune in the 1945 movie of that name?
She was a waitress who bought an eatery that she built into a chain of restaurants.

Who played Anna in *Anna and the King of Siam* (1946)? Who played the king?
Irene Dunne and Rex Harrison, respectively. It was Harrison's Hollywood debut.

>   *What was Anna's last name?*
>   In real life, it was Leonowens. In the movie, her name was Anna L. Owens.

Who took the lead parts in *The King and I* (1956)?
Deborah Kerr and Yul Brynner. Brynner won an Oscar.

Who are the three wives who receive the same letter in *A Letter to Three Wives* (1949), and who wrote it?
The recipients are Jeanne Crain, Linda Darnell, and Ann Sothern. The voice of the letter writer is provided by Celeste Holm.

Who was the first choice for the lead in *Sunset Boulevard* (1950)?
Montgomery Clift was to play Joe Gillis, the young screenwriter eventually played by William Holden.

What is the name of Bette Davis's character in *All About Eve* (1950)?

Margo Channing. Anne Baxter played her young fan and rival Eve Harrington.

Who plays the old man with the long white beard who jumps out of his bed to watch the climactic fight in *The Quiet Man* (1952)?

Francis Ford (1882–1953), brother of the movie's director, John Ford. *The Quiet Man* was Francis's twenty-ninth appearance in a John Ford film.

In what city was the waterfront in *On the Waterfront* (1954)?

New York.

For what fictitious movie did Vicki Lester (Judy Garland) win the Best Actress Oscar in *A Star Is Born* (1954)?

A World for Two.

Who played Pharaoh in *Land of the Pharaohs* (1955)?

Jack Hawkins.

What did "Marty" do for a living in the 1955 movie of that name?

Marty, played by Ernest Borgnine, was a butcher in the Bronx.

Who played the *12 Angry Men* (1957)?

The twelve jurors were played by: Henry Fonda, Lee J. Cobb, Ed Begley, E. G. Marshall, Jack Warden, Martin Balsam, John Fiedler, Jack Klugman, Edward Binns, Joseph Sweeney, George Voskovec, and Robert Webber.

Where was _Bridge on the River Kwai_ (1957) filmed?
Ceylon (now Sri Lanka).

What was Charlton Heston's number as a galley slave in _Ben-Hur_ (1959)?
Forty-one.

Who played the lead in _The Last Angry Man_ (1959)?
Paul Muni played idealistic Brooklyn doctor Sam Abelman in this film based on Gerald Green's novel.

Who looked back in anger in _Look Back in Anger_ (1959)?
Richard Burton, playing British malcontent Jimmy Porter.

What three virtues does Lentulus Batiatus (Peter Ustinov) acquire at the end of _Spartacus_ (1960)?
According to Gracchus (Charles Laughton), Batiatus acquires dignity, honesty, and courage (though Gracchus has to bribe him to acquire courage).

What was the name of the United States president in _Dr. Strangelove_ (1964)?
Merkin Muffley (Peter Sellers).

47

What was the president's name in Seven Days in
May *(1964)?*
Jordan Lyman (Fredric March).

What was the president's name in The Man *(1972)?*
Douglas Dilman (James Earl Jones).

**What role did John Wayne play in *The Greatest Story
Ever Told* (1965), director George Stevens's version of
the life of Christ?**
He played the centurion at the crucifixion. His only line
was, "Truly, this was the Son of God."

What teacher's pupils were the "crème de la crème"?
Miss Jean Brodie's (Maggie Smith's) in *The Prime of
Miss Jean Brodie* (1969).

**What was the name of the mad housewife in *Diary of
a Mad Housewife* (1970)?**
Tina Balser. She was played by Carrie Snodgress in an
Oscar-nominated performance. Her husband, Jonathan
Balser, was played by Richard Benjamin.

**Which number did Ryan O'Neal's character in *Love
Story* (1970) have after his name?**
The number IV, as in "Oliver Barrett IV." His father
was Oliver Barrett III, played by Ray Milland.

**Who requested that DJ Dave Garland (Clint East-
wood) *Play Misty for Me* (1971)?**
Jessica Walter, playing Evelyn Draper.

What was the last picture show in *The Last Picture Show* (1971)?
Red River (1948).

> *What was the name of the theater?*
> The Royal.

What was Don Corleone's phone number in *The Godfather* (1972)?
LOng Beach 4–5620. Don't bother calling it; a recording will tell you it's not in service.

What were the fates of the four main characters in *American Graffiti* (1973)?
As noted at the end of the film, John Milner (Paul LeMat) was killed by a drunken driver in December, 1964; Terry Fields (Charlie Martin Smith) was reported missing in action near An Loc in December, 1965; Steve Bolander (Ronny Howard) is an insurance agent in Modesto, California; Curt Henderson (Richard Dreyfuss) is a writer living in Canada.

How many people are killed in *Taxi Driver* (1976)?
Four: the pimp Sport; the ''timekeeper'' for Iris the prostitute; Iris's Mafioso customer; and the grocery store robber.

Who played Marilyn Monroe in the screen biography *Goodbye, Norma Jean* (1975)?
Misty Rowe. The title refers to Monroe's real name, Norma Jean Baker.

Who played the three women in Robert Altman's *Three Women* **(1977)?**
Pinky Rose (Sissy Spacek) and Milly Lammoreaux (Shelley Duvall) are fellow Texans who work in an old-age home. Willie Hart (Janice Rule) is a painter whose husband owns a motorcycle bar. The three interact.

Which Olympic Games does *Chariots of Fire* **(1981) portray?**
The 1924 Olympics in Paris.

What part did Chuck Yeager play on-screen in *The Right Stuff* **(1983)?**
He was Fred the bartender.

For what major league baseball team did Robert Redford play in *The Natural* **(1984)?**
The New York Knights.

Where was Bountiful in *A Trip to Bountiful* **(1985)?**
Texas. It was the hometown to which Mrs. Watts (Geraldine Page) wanted to return before she died.

Who were the real-life gynecologists on whose story the film *Dead Ringers* **(1988) was based?**
Steven and Cyril Marcus. The twins were found dead in their Upper East Side apartment in 1975, having killed themselves with barbiturates. In the movie, the twins were named Beverly Mantle and Elliot Mantle, both played by Jeremy Irons. Elliot was the confident, arrogant one; Beverly the shy, sensitive one.

Who is the DJ and what is the radio station in *Do the Right Thing* (1989)?
"Mister Señor Love Daddy" (Sam Jackson) is the DJ at WE LOVE radio, 108 FM—"The last on your dial, but the first in ya hearts, and that's the truth, Ruth!"

FOREIGN FILMS AND CULT FILMS

♦ ♦ ♦

What are the four "Monsieur Hulot" movies?
Monsieur Hulot's Holiday (1953), *Mon Oncle* (1958), *Playtime* (1967), and *Traffic* (1971). Monsieur Hulot was played in all four by Jacques Tati.

Who played the couple whose marriage was explored in *Scenes from a Marriage* (1973)?
Liv Ullmann and Erland Josephson played Marianne and Johan in this Ingmar Bergman film.

What are the names of the young couple played by Barry Bostwick and Susan Sarandon in *The Rocky Horror Picture Show* (1975)?
Brad Majors and Janet Weiss.

Who played Antoine Doinel in director François Truffaut's autobiographical series?
Jean-Pierre Leaud. The series consisted of: *The 400 Blows* (1959), *Love at Twenty* (1962), *Stolen Kisses* (1968), *Bed and Board* (1970), and *Love on the Run* (1979).

What are Eric Rohmer's "Six Moral Tales"?
They are:
1. *La Boulangère de Monceau* (1963)
2. *La Carrière de Suzanne* (1963).
3. *La Collectionneuse* (1967)
4. *Ma Nuit chez Maud* (1969)
5. *Le Genou de Claire* (1971)
6. *Chloe in the Afternoon/L'Amour l'après-midi* (1972)

In what French movie starring Catherine Deneuve is all the dialogue sung?
The Umbrellas of Cherbourg (1964), directed by Jacques Demy.

Did the characters in *A Man and a Woman* (1966) have names?
Yes. The man's name was Jean-Louis Duroc (Jean-Louis Trintignant). The woman's name was Anne Gauthier (Anouk Aimée).

Who is the "belle" in *Belle de Jour* (1967)?
Catherine Deneuve starred as Se'verine Se'rizy, prostitute by day, newlywed by night, in this film by Luis Buñuel.

What is François Truffaut's only film in English?
Fahrenheit 451 (1967).

What was the title of the sequel to the X-rated Swedish movie *I Am Curious (Yellow)* (1969)?
I Am Curious (Blue) (1970).

What was cult movie director Paul Bartel's first full-length feature?
Private Parts (1972), a black comedy about a hotel full of sex perverts. It featured Stanley Livingston, who played Chip on "My Three Sons" (ABC, CBS; 1960–72).

Who plays the woman with the deformed cheeks who sings about Heaven in *Eraserhead* (1978)?
Laurel Near. The music and lyrics of her song are by Peter Ivers. Fans know the character as the "Lady in the Radiator."

What director filmed the biography of Karen Carpenter entirely with dolls?
Todd Haynes. His *Superstar: The Karen Carpenter Story* (1989) was pulled from release due to legal action by the Carpenter family.

What was served at Babette's feast?
In the movie *Babette's Feast* (1987), the spread included, among other things, fresh terrapin soup, quail in vol-au-vents, blinis, caviar, and baba au rhum.

HORROR

◆ ◆ ◆

What was the first movie version of *Frankenstein*?
A 1910 version by the Edison Company featuring Charles
Ogle as the monster.

**Who played the title doctor in *The Cabinet of Dr.
Caligari* (1919)?**
Werner Krauss. Conrad Veidt played Cesare, the som-
nambulist controlled by Dr. Caligari.

**What was the name of the vampire in *Nosferatu, the
Vampire* (1922)?**
Graf Orlok, played by Max Schreck. The film, directed
by F. W. Murnau, was the first film version of Bram
Stoker's novel *Dracula,* but the name was changed to
avoid copyright problems.

Where did the idea come from for having *Franken-stein* (1931) end at a windmill?
The ending was the brainstorm of the director originally assigned to the film, Robert Florey (later replaced by James Whale). Florey's apartment was located over a Van De Kamp Bakery, whose trademark was a windmill.

What film was Boris Karloff working on when director James Whale asked him to do a screen test for *Frankenstein* (1931)?
Graft (1931), in which Karloff played a murderer. Whale spotted Karloff in the Universal commissary.

What was the mummy's name in *The Mummy* (1932)?
Im-Ho-Tep, aka Ardeth Bey, played by Boris Karloff. In the four sequels that followed—*The Mummy's Hand* (1940), *The Mummy's Tomb* (1942), *The Mummy's Ghost* (1944), and *The Mummy's Curse* (1944)—the mummy's name was Kharis. Western star Tom Tyler played Kharis in the first of the sequels; Lon Chaney, Jr., in the others.

What book was authored by Dr. Frankenstein in *Abbott and Costello Meet Frankenstein* (1948)?
The Secrets of Life and Death.

> *In* Young Frankenstein *(1974)?*
> *How I Did It.*

Who created the monster costume for *Creature from the Black Lagoon* (1954)?

Bud Westmore and Jack Kevan. Ben Chapman played the Gill-Man above water; swimming champion Ricou Browning played him underwater.

Who designed the title character in *Godzilla* (1954)?
Special effects man Eiji Tsuburaya.

What is the name of the female character slain by Norman Bates (Anthony Perkins) in *Psycho* (1960)?
Marion Crane, played by Janet Leigh. Her boyfriend is Sam Loomis (John Gavin) and her sister is Lila Crane (Vera Miles).

Who played the psychiatrist who tries to explain away Norman Bates's actions at the end of *Psycho* (1960)?
Simon Oakland played Dr. Richmond.

What Roger Corman–produced horror movies featured both Jack Nicholson and Boris Karloff?
Nicholson and Karloff appeared together in two movies filmed on the same sets, one right after the other: *The Raven* (1963) and *The Terror* (1963).

In what Japanese horror film do Mothra, Rodan, and Godzilla appear?
Ghidrah, the Three-Headed Monster (1965), directed by Inoshiro Honda.

Who played the title characters in *Billy the Kid vs Dracula* (1966)?

Chuck Courtney was Billy the Kid; John Carradine was Dracula. William Beaudine directed.

Who played the title characters in *Jesse James Meets Frankenstein's Daughter* (1966), also directed by Beaudine?
John Lupton played Jesse James, but nobody played Frankenstein's daughter. Narda Onyx played Maria Frankenstein, the baron's granddaughter.

Did the Japanese ever make a Frankenstein movie?
Yes, *Frankenstein Conquers the World* (1966).

Who played the black hero Ben in *Night of the Living Dead* (1968)?
Duane Jones.

Who trained the rats used in *Willard* (1971)?
Moe and Nora di Sesso. They were assisted by their pet cat.

Who played the boy who befriends the rat in *Ben* (1972)?
Lee Harcourt Montgomery played Danny Garrison, a boy with a heart condition and a friend of Ben.

What were the names of the 1970s British horror films that were inspired by 1950s E.C. Horror Comics? Who produced them?
Tales from the Crypt (1972) and *The Vault of Horror* (1973). Both were produced by Milton Subotsky and

Max J. Rosenberg for Amicus-Metromedia. They were released by Cinerama.

What was the name of the prehuman species resurrected in *Schlock* (1973)?
Schlockthropus. The Schlockthropus is played by twenty-two-year-old John Landis in his directorial debut. The film is also known as *The Banana Monster*.

Did Charlton Heston ever star in a horror film?
In only one—*The Awakening* (1980). He played archaeologist Matthew Corbeck in this latter-day mummy film.

What is the name of the camp terrorized by Jason in *Friday the 13th* (1980)?
Camp Crystal Lake.

What was the first slasher film to be made by women?
Slumber Party Massacre (1982), written by feminist author Rita Mae Brown, produced by Amy Jones and Aaron Lipstadt, and directed by Amy Jones.

What did "C.H.U.D." in the movie *C.H.U.D.* (1984) stand for?
Cannibalistic Humanoid Underground Dwellers.

Who supplied the voice for the gremlin Gizmo in *Gremlins* (1984)?
Howie Mandel.

Which movie based on works by Stephen King featured John Travolta?
Carrie (1976).

> *Which featured James Woods?*
> *Cat's Eye* (1985).

> *Which featured Stephen King?*
> *Creepshow* (1982). Here the author played a farmer who was slowly covered with green fungus.

MOVIE ACTORS
♦ ♦ ♦

What was the first movie featuring both John Barrymore and Lionel Barrymore?

Arsene Lupin (1932), a detective story set in Paris.

What is Katharine Hepburn's origin?

She was born on November 9, 1907, in Hartford, Connecticut. She came from a respected New England family. Her father was a surgeon and her mother a suffragette.

What was Carmen Miranda's ethnic background?

"The Brazilian Bombshell" was born in Marco de Canavezes, Portugal, in 1909. She died in 1955.

Where did Butterfly McQueen get her nickname?

Born Thelma McQueen in 1911, in Tampa, Florida, she got her nickname when she danced as a young woman in the Butterfly Ballet in a theatrical production of *A Midsummer Night's Dream*. She is best known for playing the weepy slave Prissy in *Gone With the Wind* (1939).

How many Barbara Stanwyck films have *lady* or *ladies* in the title?
Nine. They are: *Ladies of Leisure* (1930), *Ladies They Talk About* (1933), *Gambling Lady* (1934), *A Lost Lady* (1934), *The Lady Eve* (1941), *The Great Man's Lady* (1942), *Lady of Burlesque* (1943), *The Lady Gambles* (1949), and *To Please a Lady* (1950).

Of the sisters Joan Fontaine and Olivia de Havilland, whose name is real?
De Havilland's (1916–). Fontaine's (1917–) real name is Joan de Beauvoir de Havilland. Both were born in Tokyo to British parents and brought to California in childhood.

What was Lou Gehrig's only film role?
The baseball legend played himself in a western called *Rawhide* (1938). In the film, Gehrig quits baseball to retire out West, where he tangles with ranching racketeers.

Who played Auntie Em in *The Wizard of Oz* (1939)?
Clara Blandick, who often played aunts—such as Aunt Polly in *Tom Sawyer* (1930).

What were the "Scarlett Letters"?

They were letters written to David O. Selznick by hopeful unknown actresses desiring to play Scarlett O'Hara.

How many actresses interviewed for the part of Scarlett O'Hara?
There were 1,400. Four hundred were asked to do readings.

How many times did Raymond Massey play Abraham Lincoln?
Twice. In *Abe Lincoln in Illinois* (1940) and in *How the West Was Won* (1962).

In what year did Rita Hayworth's famous World War II pinup photo appear on the cover of *Life* magazine?
1941.

Where was suave, vaguely foreign Paul Henreid born?
Most famous for his role as Victor Laszlo in *Casablanca* (1942), he was born in Trieste, Italy, in 1908, but grew up in Vienna.

What did Joel McCrea regularly list as his hobby?
Acting. He listed his occupation as "rancher."

Who was "The Oomph Girl"?
Ann Sheridan.

> *Who was "The Peekaboo Girl"?*
> Veronica Lake.

Who was "The Threat"?
Lizabeth Scott.

In what year was Errol Flynn charged with statutory rape?

It was 1942. He was accused of the statutory rape of two teenage girls on his yacht. He was acquitted.

What military ranks did James Stewart and Clark Gable reach during World War II?

Stewart became an Air Force colonel, Gable an Air Force major.

Why wasn't Gregory Peck in uniform during World War II?

He was exempt from service because of a spinal injury. This helped to bring him into high demand as a leading man for films such as *Days of Glory* (1944), *The Keys of the Kingdom* (1945), and *Spellbound* (1945).

Who said, "I have decided that while I am a star I will be every inch and every moment a star. Everyone from the studio gateman to the highest executive will know it"?

Gloria Swanson.

What was Stewart Granger's real name?

James Stewart.

What was Robert Taylor's real name?

Spangler Arlington Brugh. He was born in Filley, Nebraska, in 1911.

What is Audrey Hepburn's national origin?
She was born Audrey Hepburn-Ruston near Brussels, Belgium, on May 4, 1929. Her father was an English banker and her mother a Dutch baroness.

In what movie did Audrey Hepburn play a cigarette girl?
Laughter in Paradise (UK, 1951), starring Alastair Sim and Fay Compton.

What did Paul Newman do for a living before becoming an actor?
He ran the family sporting goods store in Cleveland, Ohio. His first critical acclaim came with his Broadway debut in *Picnic* in 1953; his first screen appearance was in *The Silver Chalice* (1954).

What was Yul Brynner's national origin?
He was born on July 12, 1915, on Sakhalin, an island east of Siberia and north of Japan. In the late 1960s Brynner moved to Switzerland and became a Swiss citizen. His ancestry was part Gypsy. He died in 1985.

Who were the fathers of Rita Hayworth's two daughters?
Rebecca Welles's father was Orson Welles; Princess Yasmin Aga Khan's father was Prince Aly Khan.

How many movies did Grace Kelly make before becoming Princess of Monaco?

Eleven, beginning with a bit part in *Fourteen Hours* (1951) and ending with *High Society* (1956). Born in Philadelphia, Kelly (1928–82) married Prince Rainier III of Monaco in 1956.

Where was the exotic Cyd Charisse born?

Amarillo, Texas, in 1921. Her real name was Tula Ellice Finklea.

Where was Marlon Brando born?

Omaha, Nebraska, in 1924.

When did Lana Turner's teenage daughter, Cheryl Crane, stab Turner's boyfriend, Johnny Stompanato?

April 4, 1958.

What became of Sue Lyon after her debut as the title character in *Lolita* (1962)?

Born in 1946 in Davenport, Iowa, the actress appeared from time to time in films such as *The Night of the Iguana* (1964), *The Flim-Flam Man* (1967), *Tony Rome* (1967), *Evel Knievel* (1971), and *Alligator* (1980). She was fifteen when she played Lolita, who is twelve in the book.

How old was Marilyn Monroe when she died? What were her birth and death dates?

Thirty-six. She was born on June 1, 1926, and died of a sleeping pill overdose on August 5, 1962.

What were James Dean's birth and death dates?
He was born on February 8, 1931, and died in a car crash on September 30, 1955.

How many actors have played Marc Antony on film?
Eleven, in thirteen movies. They are:

Frank Benson—*Julius Caesar* (1911)
Henry Wilcoxon—*Cleopatra* (1934)
Charlton Heston—*Julius Caesar* (1950)
Marlon Brando—*Julius Caesar* (1953)
Raymond Burr—*Serpent of the Nile* (1953)
Helmut Dantine—*The Story of Mankind* (1957)
Georges Marchal—*Legions of the Nile* (1959—Italy, Spain, France)
Philip Saville—*An Honourable Murder* (1960—UK)
Bruno Tocci—*Caesar the Conqueror* (1962—Italy)
Richard Burton—*Cleopatra* (1963)
Sidney James—*Carry on Cleo* (1965)
Charlton Heston—*Julius Caesar* (1970)
Charlton Heston—*Antony and Cleopatra* (1972—Sweden, Spain, UK)

Who played James Bond in the movie *Casino Royale* (1967)?
David Niven. His nephew, Jimmy Bond, was played by Woody Allen.

Who said of Judy Garland's death, "She just plain wore out"?
Ray Bolger, her costar (as the Scarecrow) in *The Wizard of Oz* (1939).

Who said, "This year I'm a star, but what will I be next year—a black hole?"
Woody Allen.

Did Andy Robinson make any other movies after playing the psychotic Scorpio killer in *Dirty Harry* (1971)?
He has continued to appear in action/mystery films, including *Charley Varrick* (1973), *The Drowning Pool* (1975), and *Cobra* (1986).

Where was Jack Nicholson born?
Neptune, New Jersey, in 1937.

Did Barbara Hershey ever change her name to "Seagull"?
Yes. In 1972, at age 24, she officially changed her name to Barbara Seagull. She has since gone back to using the name "Hershey."

What product did Marilyn Chambers advertise before she starred in *Behind the Green Door* (1972)?
Her face was featured on a box of Ivory Snow.

In *American Graffiti* (1973), who was the blonde in the white T-bird?

Suzanne Somers played the woman in the white 1956 Thunderbird.

What was Piper Laurie's last film before her role as Carrie's insane mother in *Carrie* (1976)?
The Hustler (1961). Before that she had mostly played ingenues in films such as *Son of Ali Baba* (1952). She retired from movies in 1962 to marry film critic Joseph Morgenstern.

How many movies did Sylvester Stallone appear in before *Rocky* (1976)?
Eight: *A Party at Kitty and Stud's* (*The Italian Stallion*) (1970); *Bananas* (1971); *The Lords of Flatbush* (1973); *Capone* (1973); *The Prisoner of Second Avenue* (1975); *Death Race 2000* (1975); *Farewell My Lovely* (1975); *Carquake* (1975).

In what film before *Taxi Driver* (1976) did Robert De-Niro play a cabdriver?
He had a bit part as a gypsy cabdriver in *Jennifer On My Mind* (1971).

Where is the Burt Reynolds Dinner Theatre and Institute for Theatre Training located?
From its founding in 1979 until 1990, it was located in Jupiter, Florida. Since then, the Burt Reynolds Institute for Theatre Training has moved to Tequesta, Florida, while the dinner theatre (under new ownership) has become the Jupiter Dinner Theatre.

Is Sigourney Weaver any relation to old TV and movie comedian Doodles Weaver?
Yes. He was her uncle.

When did Clint Eastwood become a mayor?
He was elected mayor of Carmel-by-the-Sea, California, in 1986.

Where was Pia Zadora born and is that her real name?
Forest Hills, New York, in 1954. It is her real name.

Who is Anne Archer's mother?
Marjorie Lord, who played Kathy, the wife of Danny Williams (Danny Thomas) on "The Danny Thomas Show" (ABC, CBS, 1953–64).

What is Lena Olin's nationality?
She was born in Stockholm, Sweden, in 1955.

Who are Martha Plimpton's parents?
Keith Carradine and Shelley Plimpton. Martha Plimpton's films include *Running on Empty* (1988) and *Parenthood* (1989).

What are the names of River Phoenix's siblings?
His brother is named Leaf; his sisters are Summer, Rainbow, and Liberty. All are actors.

Are Julia Roberts and Eric Roberts related?
They are brother and sister. He is eleven years older.

What was Divine's real name?
Harris Glenn Milstead. He was born in Baltimore in 1946 and was a high school friend of John Waters, with whom he made several films. Divine died in 1989. His last film with Waters was *Hairspray* (1988), in which Divine played a housewife and mother.

What is Andy Garcia's real name?
Andres Arturo Garci-Menendez. He was born in Havana, Cuba, in 1956.

In what movies did Charlton Heston play God?
He did a voice-over as God in *The Ten Commandments* (1956). He also had an unbilled appearance as God in *Almost an Angel* (1990), starring Paul Hogan.

Who supplied the voice of Laurence Olivier in the restored bath scene in *Spartacus* (1960, restored 1991)?
Anthony Hopkins.

What is Jodie Foster's real name?
Alicia Christian Foster. She was born in 1962 in the Bronx, New York.

Where is John Wayne Airport?
Santa Ana, Orange County, California.

THE MOVIE BUSINESS
♦ ♦ ♦

Who is the Loew behind Loew's Theaters?
Marcus Loew (1870–1927), the New York–born son of
Jewish immigrants from Austria. Beginning in 1905 with
penny arcades in New York and Cincinnati, Loew's,
Inc., became one of the mightiest exhibition companies.

Where did Paramount get its mountain symbol?
The symbol originally represented a mountain from the
Wasatch Range of Utah. This was the home state of
W. W. Hodkinson, the businessman who helped found
the company in 1914.

**What three companies merged to form Metro-
Goldwyn-Mayer?**
Metro Pictures Corporation (founded 1915), Goldwyn
Pictures Corporation (1917), and Louis B. Mayer Pic-

tures (1918). The three companies merged in 1924 under the control of Loew's, Inc., the theater exhibition company.

What movie featured the credit "Script by William Shakespeare, Additional Dialogue by Sam Taylor"?
The Taming of the Shrew (1929), directed by Sam Taylor.

What movie did Universal advertise as "the strangest love story of our time"?
Dracula (1930).

What movie was advertised with the slogan "Garbo Talks"?
Anna Christie (1930), Greta Garbo's first sound film.

What happened if a movie did not meet with the requirements of the Hays Code?
The studio was fined $25,000. It might also be condemned by the Legion of Decency or boycotted. The Motion Picture Production Code (nicknamed the Hays Code for the first director of the Motion Picture Association of America [MPAA], Will H. Hays) was adopted in 1930.

When was the National Legion of Decency formed?
In 1934, by a group of Roman Catholic bishops. Through it, films were reviewed and rated for their decency. If the movie was not approved, a boycott was advised.

What were "oaters"?
Westerns, particularly low-budget Westerns.

How wide was the readership for Hedda Hopper and Louella Parsons?
At the height of their careers as newspaper columnists in Hollywood's Golden Age, they had together about seventy-five million readers.

Who came up with the slogan "Gable's Back and Garson's Got Him"?
Emily Torchia, an MGM publicist in the Culver City office. The slogan referred to *Adventure* (1945), Clark Gable's first movie after his discharge from the army during World War II. The movie also starred Greer Garson. Torchia won a bonus of $250 for the slogan.

What did one critic call "the most expensive haircut in history"?
It was the haircut of Samson (Victor Mature) by Delilah (Hedy Lamarr) in the $3 million 1949 Cecil B. DeMille epic *Samson and Delilah*.

What studio owned the copyright to the wide-screen process known as CinemaScope?
Twentieth Century-Fox.

> *What was the first film made using CinemaScope?*
> *The Robe* (1953).

> *What studio developed VistaVision?*

Paramount. The first film to use VistaVision was *Ben-Hur* (1959).

How much did *Cleopatra* cost?
The 1963 Burton-Taylor flop cost $37 million, a then unheard-of sum.

Who wrote the foreword to the first edition of Halliwell's *Filmgoer's Companion* (1965)?
Alfred Hitchcock. Leslie Halliwell, pioneer film encyclopedist, died in January, 1989.

When was Warner Brothers known as Warner Brothers-Seven Arts?
For a brief period from 1967 to 1969. It got that name when it was acquired by the Canadian-based Seven Arts Productions. In 1969, Warner Brothers became part of Kinney National Service, which later became Warner Communications.

When was the movie rating system started?
The Motion Picture Association of America started the Code and Rating Administration Board in 1968.

What movie was advertised with the line, "To avoid fainting, keep repeating: "It's only a movie . . . It's only a movie"?
The Last House on the Left (1972).

What have been the biggest-grossing movies, by decade?

1910–19 *The Birth of a Nation* (1915)
1920–29 *The Big Parade* (1925)
1930–39 *Gone With the Wind* (1939)
1940–49 *Song of the South* (1946)
1950–59 *The Ten Commandments* (1956)
1960–69 *The Sound of Music* (1965)
1970–79 *Star Wars* (1977)
1980–89 *E.T., the Extra-Terrestrial* (1982)

How many film libraries does Ted Turner own?
Three: those of RKO, MGM/UA, and Warner Brothers.

What do the following *Variety* terms mean:

webs—TV networks
pix—movies
indies—independent film distributors
b.o.—box office
boff biz—making money, doing good business
lensing—filming
thesping—acting
helming—directing

Was *Bonfire of the Vanities* the biggest box-office flop of 1990?
No. It lost only $15 million. *Havana* was the worst—it lost $35 million.

MUSIC AND MUSICALS
♦ ♦ ♦

Who turned down the lead for *The Jazz Singer* (1927)?
George Jessel.

How many times did William Powell play Florenz Ziegfeld?
Twice: in *The Great Ziegfeld* (1936), and in *Ziegfeld Follies* (1945).

What was the first film in which Andy Hardy appeared?
A Family Affair (1937), with Lionel Barrymore as Judge Hardy and Mickey Rooney as his son Andy. The Andy Hardy series began officially, however, with *You're Only Young Once* (1938), with Lewis Stone as Judge James Hardy. George B. Seitz directed most of the Andy Hardy films, including *Andy Hardy Meets Debutante* (1940),

Andy Hardy's Private Secretary (1941), *Andy Hardy's Double Life* (1942), and *Andy Hardy's Blonde Trouble* (1944). The last film was *Andy Hardy Comes Home* (1958).

How tall was the Mayor of Munchkinland in *The Wizard of Oz* (1939)?

The actor who played him, Billy Curtis, was four feet, two inches tall. Curtis (1909–1988) was also the star of the first all-little-people Western *The Terror of Tiny Town* (1938).

Who was originally supposed to play the Tin Woodsman in *The Wizard of Oz* (1939)?

Buddy Ebsen. He left the picture when he had an allergic reaction to the makeup. He was replaced by Jack Haley.

Where did Harry Lillis Crosby get the nickname "Bing"?

He got it from a comic strip he liked called "The Bingville Bugle."

Who was the "Mexican Spitfire"?

Singer Lupe Valez.

What were the first names of the Nicholas brothers?

The acrobatic dancers, who appeared in films like *Down Argentine Way* (1941), *Stormy Weather* (1943), and *The Pirate* (1948), were named Fayard and Harold Nicholas.

Where did Hollywood ice-skating clowns Frick and Frack get their names?
Werner Groebli, "Frick," took his stage name from a border town in his native Switzerland. Hansreudi Mauch, "Frack," took his name from the German word for *frock*. The team appeared in such films as *Silver Skates* (1942) and *Lady, Let's Dance* (1943).

What were the two major all-black musicals released in 1943?
Cabin in the Sky and *Stormy Weather*.

What was the name of the piano player Hoagy Carmichael portrayed in *To Have and Have Not* (1944)?
Cricket.

What was the real name of Ish Kabibble?
Merwyn A. Bogue. As "Ish," the man with the Moe Howard haircut, he did comedy with Kay Kyser and appeared in such Kyser vehicles as *Carolina Blues* (1944).

Who were *The Harvey Girls* (1946)?
They were waitresses in restaurants at railroad stations throughout the newly developing West. They were played by Judy Garland, Angela Lansbury, and Cyd Charisse.

What work was the basis for the play and movie *On the Town* (1949)?

The story of three sailors on a twenty-four-hour leave in New York City was based on the ballet *Fancy Free* by Jerome Robbins. The movie starred Gene Kelly, Frank Sinatra, and Jules Munshin.

What song tamed the savage beast in *Mighty Joe Young* (1949)?
"Beautiful Dreamer," sung by Terry Moore to the giant gorilla Joe Young. The song reappears in *Batman* (1989) as the theme song for the Joker.

What is the tongue-twister that kicks off a song-and-dance number in *Singin' in the Rain* (1952)?
"Moses supposes his toses are roses but Moses supposes erroneously."

Who were the seven brothers and the seven brides in *Seven Brides for Seven Brothers* (1954)?
The seven Pontabee brothers were:

> Adam (Howard Keel)
> Benjamin (Jeff Richards)
> Gideon (Russ Tamblyn)
> Frank (Tommy Rall)
> Daniel (Marc Platt)
> Caleb (Matt Mattox)
> Ephraim (Jacques d'Amboise)

The seven brides were:

> Milly (Jane Powell)

Liza (Virginia Gibson)
Dorcas (Julie Newmeyer [Newmar])
Alice (Nancy Kilgas)
Sarah (Betty Carr)
Ruth (Ruta Kilmonis [Lee])
Martha (Norma Doggett)

Who played Glenn Miller in *The Glenn Miller Story* (1954)?
James Stewart.

> *Who played Benny Goodman in* The Benny Goodman Story *(1955)?*
> Steve Allen.

According to the song "Think Pink" in *Funny Face* (1957), what should be done with black, blue, and beige?
Banish the black, burn the blue, and bury the beige.

Who wrote the additional songs for *Funny Face* (1957)?
Roger Edens and Leonard Gershe. The other songs were by George and Ira Gershwin.

What was the name of the pajama company in *The Pajama Game* (1957)?
Sleeptite Pajamas in Cedar Rapids, Iowa.

Who sang for Rosalind Russell in *Gypsy* (1962)?
Lisa Kirk.

Who wrote the James Bond theme?
Monty Norman and John Barry have both been credited with it.

What musical work plays during the space ballet in *2001: A Space Odyssey* (1968)?
Blue Danube Waltz by Johann Strauss.

Who sang the hit song ''Jean'' over the credits of *The Prime of Miss Jean Brodie* (1969)?
Its composer, Rod McKuen. But the single that reached *Billboard* magazine's ''Hot 100 Chart'' in 1969 was sung by folk singer Oliver.

Who wrote the lyrics of ''Suicide Is Painless,'' theme song of *M*A*S*H* (1970)?
Mike Altman, son of the film's director, Robert Altman. Johnny Mandel composed the music.

Who played the leads in *Marco* (1973), the musical adaptation of Marco Polo's journey to the Orient?
In a triumph of odd casting, Desi Arnaz, Jr., played Marco Polo and Zero Mostel played Kublai Khan.

Who played the Phantom in *Phantom of the Paradise* (1974)?
William Finley played Winslow, the Phantom, in this rock-musical version of *Phantom of the Opera*. He was stalking evil record producer Swan (Paul Williams).

Who played The Wizard of Oz in *The Wiz* (1978)?

Richard Pryor.

Who played the other leads?

Dorothy—Diana Ross
Scarecrow—Michael Jackson
Tinman—Nipsey Russell
Cowardly Lion—Ted Ross

Who composed the theme song for *Arthur* (1981)?
"Arthur's Theme (The Best That You Can Do)" required no fewer than four composers: Burt Bacharach, Carole Bayer Sager, Peter Allen, and Christopher Cross (who sang it). The song won an Oscar.

From what movie did rock group Duran Duran get its name?
From the science fiction movie *Barbarella* (1968). Duran Duran (the Concierge) was a character played by Milo O'Shea.

What about the rock group Fine Young Cannibals?
Their name came from the movie soap opera *All the Fine Young Cannibals* (1960), directed by Michael Anderson and starring Robert Wagner and Natalie Wood.

What song did Tom Hanks sing to his mother (Mercedes Ruehl) as proof her son was alive in *Big* (1988)?
"The Way We Were."

What was Marni Nixon's only film appearance?
She was a nun in *The Sound of Music* (1965). Nixon is better known for dubbing other people's singing, such as Deborah Kerr's in *The King and I* (1956), Natalie Wood's in *West Side Story* (1961), and Audrey Hepburn's in *My Fair Lady* (1964).

MYSTERY AND SUSPENSE
♦ ♦ ♦

Who played the model for the child murderer in Fritz Lang's _M_ (1931)?
Peter Kurten, middle-aged German factory worker who committed nine serial murders in Düsseldorf from 1929 to 1930. He was guillotined in 1931.

Where did Nick and Nora Charles live?
The rich bons vivants, played by William Powell and Myrna Loy in _The Thin Man_ (1934), lived in San Francisco.

What part did Walter Huston play in _The Maltese Falcon_ (1941), directed by his son John?
Captain Jacobi, the ship's officer who delivers the falcon. His role was unbilled.

Who falls from the Statue of Liberty in the climax of
***Saboteur* (1942)?**
Character actor Norman Lloyd.

Who directed the first version of *And Then There*
***Were None* (1945)?**
René Clair directed this version, starring Barry Fitzger-
ald and Walter Huston. The Agatha Christie story was
remade three times, each time as *Ten Little Indians:* in
1966 (directed by George Pollock), in 1975 (Peter Col-
linson), and in 1989 (Alan Birkinshaw).

Which actor did Raymond Chandler think gave the
best performance as Detective Philip Marlowe?
Dick Powell, in *Murder, My Sweet* (1945).

Who plays the bookstore owner with whom Philip
Marlowe (Humphrey Bogart) has a passing encounter
in *The Big Sleep* (1946)?
Dorothy Malone.

What was Alfred Hitchcock's first film in color?
Rope (1948).

Which city's streets are threatened with panic in
***Panic in the Streets* (1950)?**
New Orleans. The city is threatened by a deadly plague
which may be carried by a pair of murderers.

Where was the rear window in *Rear Window* (1954)
located?
In Greenwich Village in New York City.

In *To Catch a Thief* (1955), who extinguishes a cigarette on a plateful of eggs?
Jessie Royce Landis, who played Grace Kelly's mother in the movie.

In what movie did Doris Day first sing, "Que Sera, Sera"?
The Man Who Knew Too Much (1956), directed by Alfred Hitchcock. The song, written by Jay Livingston and Ray Evans, won an Oscar for Best Song.

What did Hitchcock consider his best MacGuffin?
Hitchcock used the word *MacGuffin* to mean a pretext for a suspense plot—an object or secret, such as military plans, of vital importance to the characters but of no real importance to the filmmaker. He thought his best MacGuffin was the set of vague "government secrets" in *North by Northwest* (1959), because this MacGuffin was "the most impertinent, the most nonexistent, and the most absurd."

What is the card that triggers the brainwashed killer's hypnotic obedience in *The Manchurian Candidate* (1962)?
The queen of diamonds.

> *What is the killer's name?*
> Raymond Shaw, played by Laurence Harvey.

Whose death leads Ira Wells (Art Carney) to team with Margo Sperling (Lily Tomlin) in *The Late Show* (1977)?

His former partner Harry Regan's (Howard Duff). Regan had been hired by Sperling to locate her missing cat.

In *Body Heat* (1981), what high school yearbook does Ned Racine (William Hurt) use to learn that Matty Walker (Kathleen Turner) is guilty of murder?
The Wheaton High School yearbook.

In *The Big Easy* (1987), what is the name of the slush fund into which police graft is being funneled?
The Widows and Orphans Fund.

What part did director Ken Russell play in *The Russia House* (1990)?
The spy master Walter.

What two horror directors appear in *The Silence of the Lambs* (1991)?
Roger Corman and George A. Romero. Jonathan Demme directed them.

OSCARS AND OTHER AWARDS

♦ ♦ ♦

What is the full name of the Academy that gives out the Academy Awards and when was it founded?
The Academy of Motion Picture Arts and Sciences is a nonprofit organization for the advancement of the film art and industry. It was founded in 1927.

How does one become a member?
By invitation only.

Who was the most nominated actor who never won an Oscar?
Richard Burton (1925–1984). He was nominated six times.

Did Lillian Gish ever receive an Oscar?

In 1970, she received a special Oscar for her cumulative work, then spanning nearly sixty years. She began making films in 1912; in 1987, she appeared in *The Whales of August*.

Who created the Academy Award statuette?

Hollywood art director Cedric Gibbons designed it. It was executed by sculptors George Stanley and Alex Smith. The statuette, then and now, is 13½ inches tall and depicts a naked man holding a sword and standing on a reel of film.

Who gave the Academy Award statuette the name "Oscar"?

A secretary named Margaret Herrick, who later became executive director of the Academy. According to legend, she looked at the statuette and said, "Why, he reminds me of my Uncle Oscar." The uncle's full name was Oscar Pierce.

Who and what received the first Academy Awards (in 1927–28) for:

Best Picture—*Wings* (1927) (Best "Production")
Best Actor—Emil Jannings in *The Last Command* (1927) and *The Way of All Flesh* (1927)
Best Actress—Janet Gaynor in *Seventh Heaven* (1927), *Street Angel* (1927), and *Sunrise* (1927)
Best Director—Frank Borzage for *Seventh Heaven* (1927)

At the 1933 awards, when Will Rogers announced, "Come and get it, Frank," and the Oscar for Best Director was not for Frank Capra, whom was it for?
For Frank Lloyd, for *Cavalcade.* Capra did not win in 1933 for *Lady for a Day,* but he won the next year for *It Happened One Night.*

Which came first, the New York Film Critics or the National Society of Film Critics?
The New York Film Critics, established 1935. The National Society of Film Critics, considered more avant-garde than the older group, was founded in 1966. Both give annual recognition to the best work in films.

When was the Cannes Film Festival established?
In 1939. Winners of its Golden Palm (for Best Film) have included *Marty* (1955), *La Dolce Vita* (1960), *M*A*S*H* (1970), and *The Tree of Wooden Clogs* (1978).

Who sponsors the Golden Globe awards?
The Hollywood Foreign Press Association, founded in 1940, an association of foreign journalists covering the Los Angeles entertainment scene. The awards were first presented in 1944, with the first Best Motion Picture award going to *The Song of Bernadette* (1943).

What movie won the Oscar for Best Picture the year *Citizen Kane* was eligible (1941)?
How Green Was My Valley.

> *The year* High Noon *was eligible (1952)?*
> *The Greatest Show on Earth.*

The year The Searchers *was eligible (1956)?*
Around the World in 80 Days.

The year Casablanca *was eligible (1943)?*
Casablanca.

Did Hoagy Carmichael ever win an Oscar for Best Song?

He won in 1951 for "In the Cool Cool Cool of the Evening," which appeared in *Here Comes the Groom,* starring Bing Crosby.

How many Oscars did Humphrey Bogart win?

One, as Best Actor for his role as Charlie Allnut in *The African Queen* (1951).

When was Best Foreign Language Film introduced as a regular category in the Academy Awards?

In 1956. The first winner was *La Strada* (Italian, 1954), directed by Federico Fellini.

What was the briefest time on-screen ever for an Oscar-winning performance?

Anthony Quinn's eight minutes on-screen as painter Paul Gauguin in *Lust for Life* (1956). Quinn won as Best Supporting Actor.

What movie made Sophia Loren famous?

Two Women (1961), for which she won an Oscar. She was also awarded a special Oscar in 1990.

Who was the first black man to win an Oscar for Best Actor?
Sidney Poitier for *Lilies of the Field* (1963).

How many Oscars has screenwriter Robert Bolt won?
Two—for *Dr. Zhivago* (1965) and for *A Man for All Seasons* (1966).

What was the most recent tie in Oscar voting for major awards?
It was in the category of Best Actress in 1968. The award went to Katharine Hepburn for *The Lion in Winter* and Barbra Streisand for *Funny Girl*.

What was the name of the woman who appeared on behalf of Marlon Brando at the 1972 Oscar telecast?
She gave her name as Sacheen Littlefeather, an "Apache," and "president of the National Native American Affirmative Image Committee." On behalf of Brando, she refused his Oscar for *The Godfather* (1972). It later turned out that Littlefeather was actually an actress named Maria Cruz. The ceremony was telecast live on March 27, 1973.

Which movie received the most Oscar nominations?
All About Eve (1950) with fourteen.

PRODUCERS

♦ ♦ ♦

What day was Louis B. Mayer's birthday?

No one knows, but he decided to make it July 4. Mayer (1885–1957) claimed he had lost the records of his real birthday during emigration from Russia. He celebrated the nation's birthday, and his own, with a big MGM picnic every Fourth of July.

Who was Louis B. Mayer's first film star?

Anita Stewart. She starred in *Virtuous Wives* (1918), the first film made by Mayer's production company, Alco (later Metro).

How many stars did MGM have in its heyday?

In 1938, it had about 120 stars and featured players under contract.

What was Universal Studios mogul Carl Laemmle doing before he got into movies?
He was the manager of the Oshkosh, Wisconsin, branch of Continental Clothing, a clothing retailer. In 1906, after losing his job in an argument with his boss, he opened a movie theater in Chicago. He soon became a film distributor and, in 1912, founded Universal. According to one account, he got the idea for the studio name from a truck that read "Universal Pipe Fittings."

What was producer Samuel Goldwyn's real name?
Samuel Goldfish. The name was first coined in 1916 when Goldfish (1882–1974) formed a company with several partners, including Edgar Selwyn (1875–1944). Fusing the names of its founders, the new company was named "Goldwyn." Goldfish liked the name so much he made it legally his own in 1918.

Who were the artists who founded United Artists?
Charlie Chaplin, D. W. Griffith, Mary Pickford, and Douglas Fairbanks. They founded this producing, releasing, and distributing company in 1919.

How many Warner brothers were there?
There were four who started the studio named Warner Brothers: Harry (1881–1958), Albert (1884–1967), Sam (1888–1927), and Jack (1892–1978). They were the children of Jewish immigrants from Poland. They founded the studio in 1923.

When was Twentieth Century-Fox formed?

In 1935, when the Fox Film Corporation, founded in 1915 by William Fox (1879–1952), merged with Twentieth Century Productions, established in 1933 by Joseph M. Schenk (1878–1961) and Darryl F. Zanuck (1902–1979).

What did the *O* in David O. Selznick (1902–1965) stand for?
Oliver.

Did Samuel Goldwyn, famous for his malapropisms, ever say, "It rolls off my back like a duck"?
No. Critic George Oppenheimer remembers coming up with this line when he was a Hollywood screenwriter. He won the commissary pool that the writers had going for the best Goldwynism of the day.

When did Dore Schary replace Louis B. Mayer as studio head of MGM?
In 1951. Schary himself was fired in 1956.

On what movies did producer Jon Peters and Barbra Streisand collaborate?
Peters produced *A Star Is Born* (1976) and coproduced (with Streisand) *The Main Event* (1979). Peters went on to team with Peter Guber to produce *Flashdance* (1983), *Rain Man* (1988), and *Batman* (1989).

What is the national origin of Merchant and Ivory, the producers of *Heat and Dust* (1983) and *A Room With a View* (1986)?

Ismail Merchant was born in 1936 in Bombay, India. James Ivory was born in 1928 in Berkeley, California. The two have collaborated since 1961.

Who produced the Al Pacino comeback vehicle *Sea of Love* (1989)?
Longtime associate Martin Bregman, who also produced the Pacino films *Serpico* (1973), *Dog Day Afternoon* (1975) and *Scarface* (1983).

PRODUCTION

♦ ♦ ♦

Who designed the electrical machinery used to create life in *Frankenstein* (1931)?
Special-effects man Ken Strickfaden.

What error appears at the end of *The Invisible Man* (1933)?
When the invisible, naked man runs through the snow, the police spot him by his footprints—but his footprints are those of shoes instead of bare feet.

How tall was the title gorilla in *King Kong* (1933)?
The six models used in the filming were each eighteen inches tall. They were made of rubber flesh and rabbit fur on a metal skeleton, and filmed in stop-motion animation. For close-ups, the filmmakers used a full-scale mechanical hand and a twenty-foot bust of Kong's head and

shoulders, covered with bear hides. Willis O'Brien created the special effects.

Did Dorothy Parker write any screenplays?
She collaborated on several, including *A Star Is Born* (1937), *The Little Foxes* (1941), *Saboteur* (1942), and *The Fan* (1949).

Who painted the backgrounds for *Gone With the Wind* (1939)?
Fitch Fulton, father of special-effects man John P. Fulton. There were about two hundred backgrounds all together.

How long did it take to make an average "B" movie in the Golden Age of Hollywood (the 1930s–1940s)?
About two weeks. Or more precisely, between twelve to eighteen days.

Where did stuntman Yakima Canutt get his name?
Born Enos Edward Canutt in the state of Washington in 1895, he acquired his stage name during his early days as a rodeo star, when a newspaper caption called him "The Cowboy from Yakima."

Who was the cinematographer on *Citizen Kane* (1941)?
Gregg Toland, who served in the same role on such classics as *The Grapes of Wrath* (1940) and *The Best Years of Our Lives* (1946).

Who is credited with the screenplay for *Citizen Kane* (1940)?
Herman J. Mankiewicz and Orson Welles.

Who is credited with the screenplay for *Gone With the Wind* (1939)?
Sidney Howard.

Who is credited with the screenplay for *Casablanca* (1942)?
Julius J. and Philip G. Epstein and Howard Koch.

What do you call props or scenery—such as barroom tables and walls—that are constructed to break easily during action sequences?
Breakaways.

What were the leeches in *The African Queen* (1951) made of?
Rubber. Designed by Cliff Richardson, they had small "blood sacs" and were stuck to Humphrey Bogart's back with waterproof adhesive.

Who developed Cinerama?
Fred Waller (1886–1954) of Paramount's special-effects department. The wide-screen process used three cameras and three projectors to record and project a single expansive image. The process debuted in 1952 with *This Is Cinerama*, a travelogue.

What was the first story feature filmed in Cinerama?
How the West Was Won (1962).

Who wrote the screenplay for *Beat the Devil* (1954)?
John Huston and Truman Capote. Huston directed.

In *The Ten Commandments* (1956), what were the "stone" tablets containing the Commandments made of?
Originally, they were made of stone, but these were too heavy for Charlton Heston (playing Moses) to carry. A new pair made of wood was used in the movie.

What error appears in the scene where Cary Grant is shot at by Eva Marie Saint in *North by Northwest* (1959)?
The shooting is supposed to be a surprise to onlookers. But in the background, a boy extra (who has rehearsed once too often) puts his fingers in his ears before the gun goes off.

What was Smell-O-Vision?
Mike Todd, Jr., introduced the aromatic cinema gimmick in 1960. Smells were directed at each individual theater seat through a tubing system activated by a "smell track" on the film. The only film made in Smell-O-Vision was *Scent of Mystery*. John Waters's "Odorama" system, introduced with *Polyester* in 1981, used a more low-tech method: scratch-and-sniff cards.

Did novelist Joseph Heller ever work in Hollywood?
Yes. With David R. Schwartz, he cowrote the screenplay of *Sex and the Single Girl* (1964), the sex farce based on Helen Gurley Brown's book of the same title. It starred

Natalie Wood, Tony Curtis, Lauren Bacall, and Henry Fonda.

How accurate was the reproduction of Fort Knox in the climax of *Goldfinger* (1964)?
The exterior set, built at Pinewood Studios in England, was accurate down to the driveway. The interior, however, was completely invented, since the filmmakers were not allowed to explore inside. Production designer Ken Adam dreamed up a set full of tubular chrome and gold piled forty feet high.

How many movie stories and screenplays did Ben Hecht write?
Alone or in collaboration, Hecht (1893–1964) wrote about seventy credited stories and scripts. He worked on many more without credit. The last film he worked on, *Casino Royale* (1967), was such a film.

How large was the brain set in *Fantastic Voyage* (1966)?
One hundred by two hundred feet and thirty-five feet high. The weblike nerve cells were made of spun fiberglass.

How did the actors wearing the ape costumes in *Planet of the Apes* (1967) breathe?
Through a specially designed passage in the ape mask's upper lip. The mask's nostrils, raised higher than those of a human nose, were non-operating. The ape makeup was designed by John Chambers.

What New York City apartment building was used as the location for *Rosemary's Baby* (1968)?
The Dakota, at Central Park West and 72 Street.

What nickname did the crew give to the mechanical shark used in *Jaws* (1975)?
"Bruce." The shark was designed by Joe Alves.

Who is the cinematographer on Jonathan Demme's movies?
Usually Tak Fujimoto. He was the cinematographer on the following Demme films:

> *Caged Heat* (1974)
> *Crazy Mama* (1975)
> *Last Embrace* (1979)
> *Melvin and Howard* (1980)
> *Swing Shift* (1984)
> *Something Wild* (1986)
> *Married to the Mob* (1988)
> *The Silence of the Lambs* (1991)

How big was the Batmobile in *Batman* (1989)?
As built by special-effects supervisor John Evans from a design by production designer Anton Furst, the car was about twenty feet long by eight feet wide. Its body was made of black fiberglass.

QUOTATIONS

♦ ♦ ♦

Who said, "Pictures are the only business where you can sit out front and applaud yourself"?
Will Rogers.

What movie first featured the line, "Do you mind if I slip into something more comfortable?"
Jean Harlow said it in *Hell's Angels* (1930).

What is the last line of *Little Caesar* (1930)?
"Mother of Mercy—is this the end of Rico?"

In what movie does Greta Garbo say, "I want to be alone"? To whom does she say it?
In *Grand Hotel* (1932), to John Barrymore.

In what movie does Bette Davis say, "I'd love to kiss you, but I just washed my hair"?
Cabin in the Cotton (1932).

Does W. C. Fields's gravestone read, "On the whole, I'd rather be in Philadelphia"?
No. In the first place, he isn't in a grave: his ashes are housed in a vault. Second, the epitaph doesn't appear there. Third, it wasn't his joke. The line first appeared in the magazine *Vanity Fair* in the 1920s. It was attributed to Fields posthumously.

In what movie does the line "The natives are restless tonight" first appear?
The Island of Lost Souls (1933). It is said by Charles Laughton.

What principle does Claudette Colbert say she's proven by revealing her leg to hitch a ride in *It Happened One Night* (1934)?
That "The limb is mightier than the thumb."

What was the first movie to feature the line "We could have made beautiful music together"?
The General Died at Dawn (1936). Gary Cooper says it to Madeleine Carroll.

In what movie is this sign posted: "Welcome to Mandrake Falls/Where the Scenery Enthralls/Where No Hardship E'er Befalls/Welcome to Mandrake Falls."?

Mr. Deeds Goes to Town (1936). The poem was written by town bard Longfellow Deeds (Gary Cooper).

What was the headline that announced James Cagney's death in the electric chair in *Angels With Dirty Faces* (1938)?
ROCKY DIES YELLOW; KILLER COWARD AT END

What was the all *K* headline in *Miracle on 34th Street* (1947)?
KRIS KRINGLE KRAZY? KOURT KASE KOMING; "KALAMITY," KRIES KIDS

How does Barbara Stanwyck say she can convince William Holden to fight in *Golden Boy* (1939)?
"I'm a dame from Newark and I know a dozen ways."

What Frank Capra character said: "The only causes worth fighting for are lost causes"?
Senator Paine (Claude Rains), long before he tried to have his state's junior senator, Jefferson Smith (James Stewart), discredited on the Senate floor in *Mr. Smith Goes to Washington* (1939).

What couple was categorized by one of its members as "bad lots both of us, selfish and shrewd, but able to look things in the eye and call them by their right names"?
Rhett Butler and Scarlett O'Hara in *Gone With the Wind* (1939). Rhett (Clark Gable) said it.

To whom was Douglas Fairbanks referring when he said, "This is one of the most fortuitous tricks in the history of civilization—that the greatest living villain in the world and the greatest comedian should look alike"?
He was referring to Adolf Hitler and Charlie Chaplin, who was getting ready to film *The Great Dictator* (1940).

Who said about Orson Welles, "There but for the grace of God goes God"?
It was supposedly said by Herman Mankiewicz, screenwriter for *Citizen Kane* (1940). But the apocryphal remark has also been attributed to Winston Churchill and Orson Welles himself.

What is James Cagney's sign-off line (as George M. Cohan) in *Yankee Doodle Dandy* (1942)?
"My mother thanks you. My father thanks you. My sister thanks you. And I thank you."

Who said, "The problems of the world are not my department. I'm a saloon keeper"?
Rick (Humphrey Bogart) in *Casablanca* (1942).

In what movie did Bette Davis say, "There comes a time in every woman's life when the only thing that helps is a glass of champagne"?
Old Acquaintance (1943).

Who asked, "Was you ever bit by a dead bee"?

Walter Brennan to nearly everyone he met in *To Have and Have Not* (1944).

Did Samuel Goldwyn say, "The next time I send a damn fool for something, I go myself"?
Director Michael Curtiz said it in disgust at a building prop person.

Who is the actor who says to Claude Rains at the end of *Notorious* (1946), "Alex, will you come in please? I wish to talk to you"?
Ivan Triesault.

Who said, "My mind is not one that grasps the immorality of the bathroom"?
Cecil B. DeMille, defending his right to film bathtub scenes.

What are the opening lines of *Sunset Boulevard* (1950)?
William Holden says, "Yes, this is Sunset Boulevard, Los Angeles, California. It's about five o'clock in the morning. That's the homicide squad—complete with detectives and newspapermen. A murder has been reported from one of those great big houses in the ten-thousand block."

Who said, "From what I hear about Communism, I don't like it because it isn't on the level"?
Gary Cooper.

To whom does Marilyn Monroe say, "I always say a kiss on the hand might feel very good, but a diamond tiara lasts forever"?
Charles Coburn in *Gentlemen Prefer Blondes* (1953).

Who said, "When you call me madam, smile"?
Ethel Merman in *Call Me Madam* (1953).

About whom was it said, "He's the kind of guy that, when he dies, he's going up to Heaven and give God a bad time for making him bald"?
Frank Sinatra. The quote is from Marlon Brando.

What did Marlene Dietrich say about the departed Orson Welles at the end of *Touch of Evil* (1958)?
"He was some kind of man. What does it matter what you say about someone?"

At what mogul's funeral is Red Skelton said to have observed, "Give the people what they want, they'll all show up"?
Harry Cohn, head of Columbia.

Who said, "With all the unrest in the world, I don't think anybody should have a yacht that sleeps more than twelve"?
Tony Curtis to hoped-for conquest Marilyn Monroe in *Some Like It Hot* (1959).

Who said, when describing his profession, "We rob banks"?

Warren Beatty (Clyde Barrow) in *Bonnie and Clyde* (1967).

Who said, "I'm a bagel on a plate of onion rolls"?
Barbra Streisand, as Fanny Brice in *Funny Girl* (1968), comparing herself to perfect chorus-line hoofers.

What gangster movie features the line, "I don't like violence, Tom. I'm a businessman. Blood is a big expense"?
The Godfather (1972). Al Lettieri as Sollozzo says it.

What is the one thing that history has taught us, according to Michael Corleone (Al Pacino) in *The Godfather, Part II* (1974)?
"That you can kill anybody."

How does John Wayne say good-bye to Kim Darby in the last line of *True Grit* (1969)?
"Well, come see a fat old man sometime!"

REMAKES AND SEQUELS
♦ ♦ ♦

What was the first name of Dr. Frankenstein in the 1931 Universal version of *Frankenstein*?
Henry, played by Colin Clive. In the book by Mary Shelley the character's name was Victor.

> *What was his son's name in* Son of Frankenstein *(1931)?*
> Wolf, as in Baron Wolf von Frankenstein, played by Basil Rathbone.

What was the name of Gene Wilder's character in *Young Frankenstein* (1974)?
Dr. Frederick Frankenstein, pronounced "FRONK-en-steen."

What was the sequel to the silent version of *The Mark of Zorro* (1925)?

Don Q, Son of Zorro (1925). Douglas Fairbanks played Don Diego Vega (Zorro) in both movies—and also Don Cesar de Vega, the son of Zorro.

How many film versions of *Holiday* have there been?
Two. The 1930 film featured Ann Harding as Linda Seton and Robert Ames as John Case—the roles taken by Katharine Hepburn and Cary Grant in the 1938 version. Edward Everett Horton played the same role in both films—Nick Potter.

What was the name of director Howard Hawks's musical remake of his own film *Ball of Fire* (1941)?
A Song Is Born (1948).

> *Who played the leads in each film?*
> *Ball of Fire*—Gary Cooper and Barbara Stanwyck;
> *A Song Is Born*—Danny Kaye and Virginia Mayo.

Of what movie was Bob Hope's *Fancy Pants* (1950) a remake?
Ruggles of Red Gap (1935), where Charles Laughton played the role later retailored for Hope.

What was the title of the 1950 remake of *To Have and Have Not* (1944)?
The Breaking Point (1950). More faithful to the Ernest Hemingway novel *To Have and Have Not*, it starred John Garfield as Harry Morgan and Patricia Neal as Leona Charles.

What is the hero dying of in the original *D.O.A.* (1950)?
Edmond O'Brien is an accountant dying of radiation poisoning (caused by iridium). In the 1988 remake, Dennis Quaid is a college professor also dying of radiation poisoning.

In the 1951 remake of *M* (directed by Joseph Losey), who took the role of the child murderer (played by Peter Lorre in Fritz Lang's 1931 version)?
David Wayne.

Who were the original angels in *We're No Angels* (1955)?
Humphrey Bogart, Aldo Ray, and Peter Ustinov were the escapees from Devil's Island.

> *Who were the angels in the 1989 film of the same title?*
> Robert DeNiro and Sean Penn.

Who starred in the remake of *My Man Godfrey* (1957)?
June Allyson took the role of madcap heiress Irene Bullock (played by Carole Lombard in the original 1936 version). David Niven took the role of Godfrey Parke, the rich man posing as a butler (played by William Powell in the original).

What was the name of the Disney movie to which *Son of Flubber* (1963) was a sequel?

The Absent-Minded Professor (1961). Both films starred Fred MacMurray as Professor Ned Brainard. Flubber, or "flying rubber," was an invention of his.

What was the last sequel to *Planet of the Apes* (1968)?
Battle for the Planet of the Apes (1973).

How many sequels did *Airport* (1970) have?
Three: *Airport 1975* (1974); *Airport '77* (1977); and *The Concorde—Airport '79* (1979), also known as just plain *Airport '79.*

> *How many of them featured George Kennedy?*
> All.

How many *Jaws* movies have there been?
Four:

> *Jaws* (1975)
> *Jaws II* (1978)
> *Jaws 3-D* (1983)
> *Jaws: The Revenge* (1987)

> *What* Jaws *movie starred Dennis Quaid?*
> The third, Jaws 3-D (*1983*).

> *Which starred Michael Caine?*
> The fourth and last, *Jaws: The Revenge* (1987).

Was there a sequel to *American Graffiti* (1973)?
Yes—*More American Graffiti* (1979). It reunited Ron Howard, Cindy Williams, Paul LeMat, Charles Martin

Smith, Candy Clark, and Mackenzie Phillips, but not Richard Dreyfuss. Rosanna Arquette and Mary Kay Place were also in it.

Who played the woman in Roger Vadim's first version of . . . *And God Created Woman* (1957)?
Brigitte Bardot.

> *Who played the woman in Vadim's 1987 . . . And God Created Woman?*
> Rebecca De Mornay.

What film was the basis for *No Way Out* (1987)?
The Big Clock (1948), set in the world of magazine publishing instead of at the Pentagon. Ray Milland played the role later taken by Kevin Costner and Charles Laughton played the Gene Hackman role.

Of what movie was Steven Spielberg's *Always* (1989) a remake?
A Guy Named Joe (1943). Richard Dreyfuss took the Spencer Tracy part and Holly Hunter took the Irene Dunne part, in this fantasy about a pilot who dies and helps another pilot romance his girlfriend.

How much did Al Pacino get for appearing in *The Godfather Part III* (1990)?
He wanted $7 million, but settled for $5 million and points when director Francis Ford Coppola threatened to begin the movie with the funeral of Michael Corleone.

SCIENCE FICTION AND FANTASY

Who wrote the music for Universal's *Flash Gordon* and *Buck Rogers* serials in the 1930s?
Franz Waxman. It is actually the same score he wrote for *The Bride of Frankenstein* (1935), often recycled in low-budget Universal productions.

Who were the warring tribes in the original *One Million B.C.* (1940)?
The Rock People, represented by Tumak (Victor Mature), and the Shell People, represented by Loana (Carole Landis). The roles were taken by John Richardson and Raquel Welch in the remake, *One Million Years B.C.* (1967).

Who played Gort, the giant robot, in *The Day the Earth Stood Still* (1951)?

Lock Martin, then the doorman at Grauman's Chinese Theatre. Director Robert Wise gave him the job because he was the tallest man he knew.

Who played the fifty-foot woman in *Attack of the Fifty Foot Woman* (1958)?
Allison Hayes.

On what day does *The Time Machine* (1960) open?
December 31, 1899.

In what movie did Japanese star Toshiro Mifune play Sinbad?
The Lost World of Sinbad (1963).

What was the name of the submarine injected into the scientist's body in *Fantastic Voyage* (1966)?
The *Proteus*.

Who were the cinematographers on *2001: A Space Odyssey* (1968)?
Geoffrey Unsworth and John Alcott. Alcott was also Kubrick's cinematographer on *A Clockwork Orange* (1971), *Barry Lyndon* (1975), and *The Shining* (1980).

How big was the model of the spaceship Discovery *used in* 2001: A Space Odyssey *(1968)?*
The main model was 54 feet long. It was filmed moving along a track 150 feet in length. A smaller, 15-foot model was used for some shots.

What was the name of the spaceship in *Silent Running* (1971)?

The *Valley Forge*. It got its name from the location used for filming some of its interiors—a decommissioned aircraft carrier called the U.S.S. *Valley Forge*.

What was Princess Leia Organa's (Carrie Fisher's) home planet in *Star Wars* (1977)?

Alderaan.

According to the opening titles, which episode of a fictitious serial is *Star Wars* (1977)?

"Episode IV: A New Hope."

What movie inspired *Alien* (1979)?

It! The Terror from Beyond Space (1958). Both movies were about a spaceship with an alien stowaway.

What was Steven Spielberg's working title for *E.T.* (1982)?

A Boy's Life.

What were the renegade androids in *Blade Runner* (1982) called?

Replicants. "Blade runners" were the people assigned to hunt them down.

What is the name of the "no-win" test that Lieutenant Saavik (Kirstie Alley) fails at the beginning of *Star Trek II: The Wrath of Khan* (1982)?

The Kobayashi Maru.

How many directors worked on *Twilight Zone—The Movie* (1983)?
Four: John Landis, Steven Spielberg, Joe Dante, and George Miller.

Who else died with actor Vic Morrow during the filming of *Twilight Zone—The Movie* (1983)?
Two Vietnamese extras, six-year-old Renee Chen and seven-year-old Myca Dinh Lee. All were killed while a helicopter scene was being shot for the segment by John Landis.

What is the name of the Devil as played by Jack Nicholson in *The Witches of Eastwick* (1987)?
Daryl Van Horne.

Who plays the young Jack Nicholson in *Batman* (1989)?
Young Jack Napier (the character who later becomes the Joker) is played by Hugo E. Blick.

Who was originally cast as Vicki Vale in *Batman* (1989)?
Sean Young, who fractured her shoulder in a riding accident two weeks before the start of principal filming. Kim Basinger took over.

To whom does Quaid (Arnold Schwarzenegger) say, "Consider that a divorce" in *Total Recall* (1990)?
His wife Lori (Sharon Stone), upon killing her.

SILENT FILMS

♦ ♦ ♦

How long was Dorothy Gish's film career?

She started making movies with *An Unseen Enemy* in 1912 and ended with *The Cardinal* in 1963.

Who was older, Dorothy Gish or Lillian Gish?

Lillian, by almost two years. Lillian was born in 1896; Dorothy was born in 1898 and died in 1968.

How much was the option on Thomas Dixon, Jr.'s *The Klansman*, the book on which *The Birth of a Nation* (1915) was based?

D. W. Griffith paid $2,500 for the rights. Dixon also received a twenty-five percent interest on the picture, which brought him several million dollars. *The Birth of a Nation* also drew on Dixon's novel *The Leopard's Spots*.

How much money did an average silent movie star make?

Movie acting was well-paying, even then. For example, in 1913, when Mary Pickford was starting out, she made $500 per week. In 1916, after she had become "America's Sweetheart," she commanded $10,000 per week, plus bonuses.

What was Rudolph Valentino's real name?

Rodolfo Alfonzo Raffaele Pierre Philibert Guglielmi d'Antonguolla, born on May 6, 1895, in Castellaneta, Italy.

Where did Theda Bara get her name?

The silent vamp's name was an anagram for "Arab Death." She was born Theodosia Goodman.

Whom was Fatty Arbuckle accused of killing?

Virginia Rappé. Roscoe "Fatty" Arbuckle was accused of killing her in a drunken stupor after a Labor Day party in San Francisco in 1921, but he was acquitted of criminal charges.

Where was the whaling movie _Down to the Sea in Ships_ (1922) shot?

On location in the traditional home of New England whalers—New Bedford, Massachusetts.

Who played the object of Lon Chaney's affections in _The Phantom of the Opera_ (1925)?

Mary Philbin was Christine Daae, protégée of Erik, the Phantom (Chaney).

Who played *The Merry Widow* (1925)? Whose widow was she?
Mae Murray played the title role in this film directed by Erich von Stroheim. Her character, Sally O'Hara, was the widow of Baron Sadoja (Tully Marshall).

With whom does Charlie Chaplin share a cooked boot in *The Gold Rush* (1925)?
Mack Swain, playing Big Jim McKay.

Who played the title role in the 1926 *Ben-Hur*?
Ramon Novarro played Judah Ben-Hur, with Francis X. Bushman as his friend-turned-enemy Messala. Fred Niblo directed.

> *Who took the roles in the 1959 remake?*
> Charlton Heston and Stephen Boyd, respectively. William Wyler directed.

What did the *X* in Francis X. Bushman's name stand for?
Xavier.

Who played Gatsby in the first, silent version of *The Great Gatsby* (1926)?
Warner Baxter. Lois Wilson played Daisy Buchanan.

Who was the temptress in *The Temptress* (1926)?
Greta Garbo as Elena.

What movie made Clara Bow the "It" Girl?
It was the 1927 movie *It,* directed by Clarence Badger and Josef von Sternberg. Bow's character was named Betty Lou.

Whose face was so unforgettable in the title role of *The Passion of Joan of Arc* (1928)?
Falconetti (Marie Falconetti, 1901–46), a French stage actress, starred in this film by Carl Dreyer. This was Falconetti's only film.

Were the films of silent film director John Waters anything like those of his present-day namesake?
No. Silent film director John Waters was responsible for formula Westerns like *Nevada* (1927), starring Gary Cooper and Thelma Todd. Present-day cult movie director John Waters is responsible for offbeat works like *Pink Flamingos* (1972) and *Hairspray* (1988).

How much did the studios spend on converting their filming structures to sound stages?
Between June 1928 and December 1929, the major studios spent about thirty-seven million dollars.

What was the last completely silent film?
The last American movie without a soundtrack released for general distribution was *The Poor Millionaire* (1930), directed by George Melford and starring Richard Talmadge. A few later films, such as *City Lights* (1931), featured synchronized music and sound effects but no spoken dialogue.

TEAMS

♦ ♦ ♦

When were George Burns and Gracie Allen married?
In 1926. Their marriage lasted until Gracie's death in 1965.

How did John Ford, John Wayne, and Ward Bond start making movies together?
In the 1920s, John Wayne was a University of Southern California student who worked as a laborer and bit player on the Fox lot, where he got to know director John Ford. In 1929, Wayne and fellow USC football player Ward Bond came out to Annapolis with the entire USC football team to appear in Ford's movie about the Naval Academy, *Salute*. The three remained friends and collaborators from then on.

How long were Joel McCrea and Frances Dee married?

Fifty-seven years, from 1933 to his death in 1990. They appeared together in films like *Wells Fargo* (1937) and *Four Faces West* (1948).

What was the first film to pair Boris Karloff and Bela Lugosi?
The Black Cat (1934).

In how many movies did Robert Taylor and Barbara Stanwyck appear together?
Three: *His Brother's Wife* (1936), *This Is My Affair* (1937), and *The Night Walker* (1965). The two were married in 1939 and divorced in 1952.

Lucille Ball and Desi Arnaz met on the set of which movie?
Too Many Girls (1940), produced by RKO and directed by George Abbott.

What movie duo was known by the nicknames "The Singing Capon" and "The Iron Butterfly"?
Nelson Eddy and Jeanette MacDonald.

Who was William Randolph Hearst's extramarital love interest, the model for Susan Alexander in *Citizen Kane* (1941)?
Marion Davies, an actress for whom Hearst founded a movie production company, Cosmopolitan Pictures (which was absorbed by MGM in 1925).

In how many movies did Humphrey Bogart, Mary Astor, and Sydney Greenstreet star together?
Two—*The Maltese Falcon* (1941) and *Across the Pacific* (1942). Both were directed by John Huston.

How many times had Humphrey Bogart been married when he met Lauren Bacall?
Before he met Bette Joan Perske (aka Lauren Bacall), he had been married three times: first, to Helen Menken, then to Mary Philips, both actresses. These marriages had ended in divorce. When he met Bacall on the set of *To Have and Have Not* (1944), he was married to Mayo Methot.

In how many movies did Humphrey Bogart and Lauren Bacall appear together?
Five. *To Have and Have Not* (1944); *The Big Sleep* (1946); *Dark Passage* (1947); *Key Largo* (1948); and *Two Guys from Milwaukee* (1946), in which they played themselves in an unbilled appearance.

Who is older, Paul Newman or Joanne Woodward?
Newman. Newman was born in 1925, Woodward in 1930.

What was Annette Funicello's and Frankie Avalon's first movie together?
Beach Party (1963).

> *Who was their arch-nemesis in that film?*
> It was Eric Von Zipper, the would-be tough biker, played by Harvey Lembeck.

How many husbands did Judy Garland have, besides Vincente Minnelli?

Four. The five husbands were: David Rose, Vincente Minnelli, Sid Luft, Mark Herron, and Mickey Deans. She was married to Minnelli from 1945 to 1951.

Who played C-3PO and R2-D2 in *Star Wars* (1977)?

The comedy team of robots was played by Anthony Daniels (C-3PO) and Kenny Baker (R2-D2).

When was Isabella Rossellini married to director Martin Scorsese?

From 1979 to 1982. Afterward, she became the companion of director David Lynch.

What movies teamed Jeff Goldblum and Geena Davis?

Married in 1987 and separated in 1990, the two actors met on the set of *Transylvania 6-5000* (1985). Their other collaborations were *The Fly* (1986) and *Earth Girls Are Easy* (1989).

How many wives did Cary Grant have?

Five: Virginia Cherrill, Barbara Hutton, Betsy Drake, Dyan Cannon, and Barbara Harris.

How long were Gene Wilder and Gilda Radner married?

From 1984 until her death from cancer in 1989.

Who is older, Hume Cronyn or Jessica Tandy?

Tandy, by two years. Cronyn was born in 1911, Tandy in 1909.

How many movies have actor Robert Redford and director Sydney Pollack made together?
Seven: *This Property Is Condemned* (1966); *Jeremiah Johnson* (1972); *The Way We Were* (1973); *Three Days of the Condor* (1975); *The Electric Horseman* (1979); *Out of Africa* (1987); and *Havana* (1990).

Who are the most married Hollywood stars?
Zsa Zsa Gabor, Stan Laurel, Mickey Rooney, Elizabeth Taylor, and Lana Turner have each been married eight times.

WESTERNS

♦ ♦ ♦

Where did John Wayne get the nickname "Duke"?
He had a dog named "Duke" as a child. To distinguish them, the dog was known as "Big Duke" and Wayne as "Little Duke."

Where did Western actor Guinn "Big Boy" Williams get his nickname?
Will Rogers called him that for his large size. Williams supported Rogers in movies like *Almost a Husband* (1919).

Who was the first Jesse James on-screen?
His son—Jesse James, Jr. James's movies include: *Jesse James Under the Black Flag* (1921) and *Jesse James as the Outlaw* (1921), both silent films.

What movie was billed as "the first 100% all-talking drama filmed outdoors"?

The 1929 Western *In Old Arizona*, for which Warner Baxter won the Best Actor Oscar.

What were Gene Autry's "Ten Commandments of a Cowboy"?

1. A cowboy never takes unfair advantage—even of an enemy.
2. A cowboy never betrays a trust.
3. A cowboy always tells the truth.
4. A cowboy is kind to small children, to old folks, and to animals.
5. A cowboy is free from racial and religious prejudice.
6. A cowboy is helpful, and when anyone's in trouble he lends a hand.
7. A cowboy is a good worker.
8. A cowboy is clean about his person and in thought, word, and deed.
9. A cowboy respects womanhood, his parents, and the laws of his country.
10. A cowboy is a patriot.

What were the real names of the following Western actors:

Slim Pickens—Louis Bert Lindley, Jr.
Roy Rogers—Leonard Slye
Gene Autry—Gene Autry
Tom Mix—Thomas Mix
Hoot Gibson—Edmund Richard Gibson

Allan "Rocky" Lane—Harold Albershart
Will Rogers—William Penn Adair Rogers

Where was the stagecoach going in the 1939 movie Stagecoach?
From Tonto, New Mexico, to Lordsburg, Arizona.

Did Fritz Lang ever direct a Western?
Three—*The Return of Jesse James* (1940), *Western Union* (1941), and *Rancho Notorious* (1952).

What is the brand that Tom Dunson (John Wayne) draws at the end of *Red River* (1948)?
A river with a *D* on the top and an *M* on the bottom. The *D* is for Dunson, the *M* is for Matthew Garth (Montgomery Clift). Dunson tells Garth, "You've earned it."

In what Western did John Wayne say, "Don't apologize. It's a sign of weakness"?
In *She Wore a Yellow Ribbon* (1949), in the character of Captain Nathan Brittles. He was upbraiding one of his soldiers.

What movie was advertised with the line, "She's got the biggest six-shooters in the West!"
The Beautiful Blonde from Bashful Bend (1949), starring Betty Grable.

When Joey (Brandon DeWilde) calls out to Shane (Alan Ladd), "Come back!", where is Shane supposed to come back to?

A ranch in the Grand Tetons, Wyoming, in the movie *Shane* (1953).

Who was *The Man Who Shot Liberty Valance* (1962)?
It was not the man given credit for it, Senator Ransom Stoddard (James Stewart). It was Tom Doniphon (John Wayne), a relic of an older, less civilized West.

In what movies did the following actors play Indians:

Linda Darnell—*Buffalo Bill* (1944)
Burt Lancaster—*Apache* (1954)
Audrey Hepburn—*The Unforgiven* (1960)
Paul Newman—*Hombre* (1967)

Who was the Cincinnati Kid?
Steve McQueen in the 1965 movie of the same name.

> *The Ringo Kid?*
> John Wayne in *Stagecoach* (1939).

> *The Waco Kid?*
> Gene Wilder in *Blazing Saddles* (1974).

Did Paul Newman ride the bicycle himself in *Butch Cassidy and the Sundance Kid* (1969)?
Yes. There was no double.

In *The Last Picture Show* (1972), who was Sam the Lion?

The owner of the pool hall in Anarene, Texas, was played by veteran Western actor Ben Johnson. His performance earned him an Oscar for Best Supporting Actor.

What was the name of *The Shootist* (1976)?
Played by John Wayne, he was John Bernard Brooks. It was Wayne's last film.

What part does country singer Randy Travis play in *Young Guns* (1988)?
He is a ring member.

What Indian language is spoken in *Dances With Wolves* (1990)?
Lakota, the language of the Sioux.

How many films did John Ford shoot in Monument Valley, on the Arizona-Utah line?
Nine.

PART·II
◆ TELEVISION ◆

CHILDREN'S TELEVISION
♦ ♦ ♦

Who was television's first teen star?
Don Hastings, the teenager who played the Video Ranger, sidekick of "Captain Video" (DuMont, 1949–55).

Who played "Tom Corbett, Space Cadet"?
Frankie Thomas played the lead in this rival to "Captain Video" (DuMont, 1949–55). "Tom Corbett, Space Cadet" ran from 1950 to 1955 and aired successively on all four networks—CBS, ABC, NBC, and DuMont.

Who provided the voice of Winky Dink in "Winky Dink and You" (CBS, 1953–57; syndicated, 1969–75)?
Mae Questel, better known as the voice of Betty Boop.

How much did a Winky Dink TV Kit cost?

Fifty cents bought a plastic sheet and magic crayons to use on your television set during the show.

Who else appeared on "Howdy Doody" (NBC, 1947–60) besides Buffalo Bob and Howdy Doody?
There was an entire family of performers under Buffalo Bob (Bob Smith) and Howdy Doody. They included Clarabell the Clown (Bobby Nicholson), the Princess (Judy Tyler), and Chief Thunderthud (Bill Lecornec). Howdy was operated by Lee Carney.

How many children sat in the Peanut Gallery on "Howdy Doody"?
Only fifty at a time.

What are the complete names of Rocky, Bullwinkle, Boris, and Natasha?
Rocket J. Squirrel, Bullwinkle J. Moose, Boris Badenov, and Natasha Fatale. "The Bullwinkle Show" aired on ABC (and later NBC) from 1959 to 1963 in 147 episodes.

Who provided the voice for Rocky the Flying Squirrel on "The Bullwinkle Show" (ABC, NBC, 1959–1963)?
Voice expert June Foray, who also provided the voices on the show for Dudley Do-Right's girlfriend Nell, and for others.

Where did Bullwinkle J. Moose live?
Frostbite Falls, Minnesota.

According to "The Flintstones" (ABC, 1960–66) theme, how did the Flintstone family car run?
Through the courtesy of Fred's two feet.

Who was Yogi Bear ("The Yogi Bear Show"; synd., 1961–63) smarter than?
The average bear.

When was the "Top Cat" series on prime-time TV?
In the 1961–62 season, on Wednesday nights from 8:30 to 9:00 P.M., on ABC.

Who provided the voice of Jane Jetson in the original run of "The Jetsons" (ABC, 1962–63)?
Penny Singleton, who played Blondie in the *Blondie* film series that ran from 1938 to 1950.

Who led the Young People's Concerts?
Leonard Bernstein, for CBS.

What was Mr. Magoo's complete name?
Quincy Magoo. His voice in the 1964–65 comedy series, "The Famous Adventures of Mr. Magoo" (NBC), was provided by Jim Backus.

What is the name of the puppet-king in "Mister Rogers' Neighborhood" (PBS, 1965–)?
King Friday XIII.

Where do "The Simpsons" (Fox, 1989–) live?
In a town called Springfield.

COMMERCIALS

♦ ♦ ♦

What product did Eleanor Roosevelt endorse on TV?
Good Luck Margarine. She was paid $35,000 for the endorsement.

What company's products did Henry Fonda endorse on TV?
GAF.

> *Robert Young?*
> Sanka.

> *Andy Griffith?*
> Maxwell House.

When did Old Gold cigarette packs start dancing in TV commercials?

In 1950, in a spot called "Dancing Butts." Women wearing huge Old Gold packages did the dancing.

Where did Dow Chemical originally concentrate its Saran Wrap commercials?
On "Today" in the early 1950s. Dave Garroway would hold up a piece of the wrap to demonstrate how clear it was.

What is the name of the Alka-Seltzer mascot?
Speedy, a puppet, who has been around since 1953.

When did Mabel first advertise Carling Black Label Beer?
The cartoon character first appeared in 1954.

What razor could shave "the short, close fuzz of a peach without harming its tender skin"?
A Remington electric shaver, in 1954, long before Victor Kiam bought the company.

What were the names of the Piels Beer drinkers whose voices were provided by Bob Elliott and Ray Goulding?
Bert and Harry, the "Piels Brothers." The ad first appeared in 1955.

When did a cartoon child first cry, "I want my Maypo"? What is Maypo?
The animated ad first aired in 1956. Maypo is a maple-flavored oatmeal, new at the time.

What did Winston taste good "like," and when did it first do so on TV?

It tasted good "like a cigarette should." The first commercial using the jingle appeared in 1956.

What was the first product advertised by the Muppets?

Wilkins Coffee, in 1957. The Muppets were featured in an eight-second commercial in which one Muppet fires a cannon at another to prevent him from drinking his Wilkins coffee.

In what ear does Mr. Clean wear his earring?

The gold hoop is in his left earlobe. Mr. Clean made his first TV appearance in 1958. The Mr. Clean jingle was sung by Don Cherry and Betty Bryan.

When did a happy child first report, "Look, Ma, no cavities!" because of Crest Toothpaste?

In 1958.

What was the name of the man who played El Exigente in Savarin Coffee commercials in the 1960s and 1970s?

He was Carlos Montalban, brother of actor Ricardo Montalban. Born in 1904, he died in 1991.

Who played Josephine the Plumber? What did she advertise?

Jane Withers was Josephine, who sang the praises of Comet Cleanser in the 1960s.

In the 1960s, who coaxed men to "take it off" with Noxzema shave cream?
Gunilla Knutson, to the strains of "The Stripper."

What pizza product did the Lone Ranger and Tonto endorse?
In the 1960s, Clayton Moore and Jay Silverheels (The Lone Ranger and Tonto, respectively) advertised Jeno's Pizza Rolls.

Did Jesse White, famed as the lonely Maytag Repairman, ever play parts on TV series?
He appeared regularly on three series: "Private Secretary" (CBS, NBC, 1953–57), "The Danny Thomas Show" (ABC, CBS, 1953–64), and "The Ann Sothern Show" (CBS, 1958–61).

Who was Mason Reese?
Born in 1966, the red-haired, round-faced Reese was perhaps the most widely seen child in TV commercials in the early 1970s. He started making commercials in 1970, and won three Clios. He advertised, among other products, Oscar Mayer bologna. He was also a favorite guest on "The Mike Douglas Show" (synd., 1963–82).

Who was Mother Nature in the Parkay Margarine campaign, "It's not nice to fool Mother Nature"?
Dena Dietrich. She also appeared in TV series such as "Adam's Rib" (ABC, 1973) and "The Ropers" (ABC, 1979–80).

Who asked, ''Where's the beef?''

Clara Peller asked it for Wendy's, and Walter Mondale asked it in the 1984 presidential campaign.

Who played Joe Isuzu?

David Leisure was the pathological liar in the 1980s Isuzu car commercials. He has also appeared on the TV sitcom ''Empty Nest'' (NBC, 1988–).

DRAMA

♦ ♦ ♦

What was the first prime-time soap opera?
Appearing long before "Peyton Place" (ABC, 1964–69), it was "A Woman to Remember," starring Patricia Wheel. The series, which was based on a daytime serial, ran on the DuMont network from May to July, 1949.

Who introduced the first episode of "Gunsmoke" (CBS, 1955–75)?
John Wayne. On September 10, 1955, Wayne explained that he was not able to star in the show, but had recommended a young actor named James Arness for the part of Marshal Matt Dillon.

Was *Casablanca* (1942) ever turned into a TV series?

Yes, twice. In the 1955–56 season, "Casablanca" (ABC) was a short-lived thirty-minute series starring Charles McGraw as Rick Jason (changed from Rick Blaine). In 1983–84, ABC attempted another "Casablanca." Rick Blaine was played by David Soul.

What was Clint Eastwood's character named in "Rawhide"?

He was Rowdy Yates on the CBS Western that ran from 1959 to 1966.

Where was the Ponderosa ranch in "Bonanza" (NBC, 1959–73)?

Near Virginia City, Nevada.

What was the age order of the Cartwright sons?
From oldest to youngest, they were:

Adam (Pernell Roberts)
Eric "Hoss" (Dan Blocker)
Joseph "Little Joe" (Michael Landon)

What symbols appeared at the beginning of "Ben Casey" (ABC, 1961–66)?

Man, Woman, Birth, Death, Infinity.

What was the Fugitive's name ("The Fugitive," ABC, 1963–67)?

Dr. Richard Kimble, played by David Janssen.

What was the name of the One-Armed Man on "The Fugitive" (ABC, 1963–67)?
Fred Johnson, played by Bill Raisch.

> *When was he captured?*
> In the final episode, which aired on August 29, 1967.

What was the name of the bear that played "Gentle Ben" (CBS, 1967–69)?
Bruno.

Who played "Alias Smith and Jones" (ABC, 1971–73)?
Peter Deuel (aka Duel) played Hannibal Heyes (alias Joshua Smith) and Ben Murphy played Jed "Kid" Curry (alias Thaddeus Jones). After Deuel died of an apparent suicide, Roger Davis took over the role of Smith.

What was the time setting of the last episode of "The Waltons" (CBS, 1972–81)?
D-Day, June 6, 1944. The series began with a pilot film, "The Homecoming" (CBS, 1971), set during Christmas, 1933.

Who served as the grown-up voice of John-Boy, narrating "The Waltons" (CBS, 1972–81)?
Earl Hamner, Jr., the show's co-executive producer, who based the series on his own recollections of growing up in rural Virginia. Richard Thomas played the young John-Boy.

Who serves as the grown-up voice of Kevin Arnold, narrating "The Wonder Years" (ABC, 1988–)?
Daniel Stern, who played a burglar in *Home Alone* (1990) and a bicyclist in *Breaking Away* (1979). Fred Savage plays the young Kevin Arnold.

What show did "Gunsmoke" (CBS, 1955–75) spin off?
"Dirty Sally" (CBS, 1974).

How many episodes of "Gunsmoke" (CBS, 1955–75) were there?
Six hundred and thirty-five—409 of them in black and white, 226 in color. The show was the longest-running weekly prime-time series with continuing characters.

Where in Dallas was "Dallas" (CBS, 1978–91) set?
It was not set in Dallas, but nearby in rural Braddock, Texas. The Ewing ranch there was called Southfork.

What season of "Dallas" (CBS, 1978–91) was a dream?
The 1984–85 season. It was revealed to have been a dream of Pam Ewing to explain the reappearance of her husband Bobby (Patrick Duffy), previously killed off.

What was the real name of the hospital nicknamed "St. Elsewhere" (NBC, 1982–86)?
St. Eligius in Boston. It received its nickname because other hospitals dumped their unwanted patients there.

What was the name of Hope and Michael Steadman's dog on "thirtysomething" (ABC, 1987–91)? What were the names of their children?
Grendel, Janie, and Leo, respectively.

What song introduced each episode of "China Beach" (ABC, 1988–91)?
"Reflections," by Diana Ross and the Supremes.

What is the population of "Twin Peaks" (ABC, 1990–91)?
According to the sign that flashes on the screen in the opening credits of the series, it is 51,201.

What is the population of Cicely, Alaska, setting of "Northern Exposure" (CBS, 1990–)?
815.

Who killed Laura Palmer (on "Twin Peaks," ABC, 1990–91)?
Her father, Leland Palmer (Roy Wise), while possessed by an evil spirit named Bob. Laura Palmer was played by Sheryl Lee.

NEWS, SPORTS, AND WEATHER

♦ ♦ ♦

What was the first TV news show to feature newsreel footage?

"The Camel News Caravan" (NBC, 1949–56), with John Cameron Swayze. Before then TV news relied mainly on announcers.

What was the first inauguration to be televised?

Harry S. Truman's, in January 1949.

What was the first televised baseball game?

It was a May 1939 game between Columbia and Princeton.

When did NBC begin national nightly newscasts?

In April 1944.

> *CBS?*
> In May 1948, read by Douglas Edwards.

> *ABC?*
> In August 1948, read by H. R. Baukhage and Jim Gibbons.

How long did the original "Roller Derby" run?

The hugely popular show ran on ABC for two years, from March 1949 to August 1951.

When did the Estes Kefauver investigations run?

The investigations of politics and crime began in 1951, and like the Watergate investigations in the early 1970s, were broadcast during the day.

When did the "Today" show premiere?

January 14, 1952, on NBC, broadcasting from New York. The host was Dave Garroway.

> *What was Garroway's sign-off line?*
> "Peace."

When did chimpanzee J. Fred Muggs join the "Today" (NBC, 1952–) cast?

In January 1953. Ratings immediately soared. Muggs was let go four years later when he got too old and hard to handle. NBC said that Muggs had "decided to terminate'' his position so he could ''extend his personal horizons.''

What was the wrestler Gorgeous George's real name?
George Wagner.

When did Chet Huntley and David Brinkley first team up?
For the 1956 presidential conventions. Their patter led to places as anchormen of the NBC nightly news that fall. Their show was called ''The Huntley-Brinkley Report'' (1956–71).

Who started the practice of blacking out home baseball game telecasts?
Walter O'Malley, owner of the Dodgers, when he moved the team from Brooklyn to Los Angeles in 1957.

When was the first Nixon-Kennedy debate?
The first of the four debates was held on September 26, 1960, in Chicago. Howard K. Smith was the moderator. The panel included Robert Fleming (ABC), Stuart Novins (CBS), Sander Vanocur (NBC), and Charles Warren (Mutual Radio).

What did Jim McKay do before ''ABC's Wide World of Sports'' (1961–)?
He appeared on several shows for ABC—''Sports Spot'' (1951), ''Make the Connection'' (1955), and ''The Verdict Is Yours'' (1958). In 1961, he appeared on ''Wide World of Sports'' and has never left.

How long was Walter Cronkite anchor of the "CBS Evening News"?
Cronkite could be heard intoning "And that's the way it is . . ." from April 16, 1962, to March 6, 1981.

What time was the announcement of President Kennedy's assassination made on TV?
It was at 1:40 P.M. EST on Friday, November 22, 1963. On CBS, "As the World Turns" was interrupted by Walter Cronkite with the news bulletin. Actress Helen Wagner had just been saying, "I gave it a great deal of thought, Grandpa," when the episode was cut off.

How long has William F. Buckley's syndicated talk show "Firing Line" been on the air?
Since April 1966.

How long has Charles Kuralt's "On the Road" feature appeared on "The CBS Evening News"?
Since October 1967.

Who were the athletes who raised their fists in a "black power" salute at the 1968 Summer Olympics?
Sprinters Tommie Smith and Juan Carlos, winners of medals in the 200-meter event. The 1968 Olympics from Mexico City were televised in the United States on ABC.

Who did CBS's news commentary on July 20, 1969, the day of the first moon landing?
Walter Cronkite, astronaut Wally Schirra, and science fiction writer Arthur C. Clarke (author of *2001*).

Who said, "I do not understand Don Meredith and I never will"?
Howard Cosell, his broadcasting partner on ABC's "Monday Night Football" in 1970–73 and 1977–83.

Who were the original hosts of "NFL Monday Night Football" (ABC, 1970–)?
Howard Cosell and Don Meredith.

When did Billie Jean King play Bobby Riggs?
ABC telecast the match at 8:00 P.M. on September 20, 1973. It was played in the Astrodome in Houston. The prize was $100,000. King won the five-set match.

What is the "ten-minute ticker"?
A rule devised by Michael Weisman, NBC Sports producer, requiring production assistants covering a game to update the scores for other games every ten minutes.

Who was the first host of "Good Morning America" (ABC, 1975–)?
David Hartman.

Who was the first female national news anchor?
Barbara Walters. She cohosted "The ABC Evening News" with Harry Reasoner from 1976 to 1978.

Where was Ted Koppel born?
Lancashire, England, in 1940. He has hosted ABC's "Nightline" since 1979.

Where was Peter Jennings born?
In Toronto, Canada, in 1938. He anchored the "ABC Evening News" from 1965 to 1968. He became co-anchor of ABC's "World News Tonight" in 1978, and sole anchor in 1983.

Who was the first president whom Sam Donaldson covered as ABC's White House correspondent?
Jimmy Carter, beginning in 1977. By the time Carter's term was over, the departing president wished two bad things on his successor: Menachem Begin and Sam Donaldson.

When did Willard Scott join the "Today" cast (NBC, 1952–)?
In March 1980. Before then he was the weatherman at NBC's Washington affiliate.

When were the Goodwill Games first held?
In July 1986, in Moscow. The brainchild of Ted Turner, the games included events such as basketball, boxing, gymnastics, track and field, and wrestling.

What are the first names of the people behind "Agronsky and Company" (synd., 1969–87) and "The McLaughlin Group" (synd., 1982–)?
Martin Agronsky and John McLaughlin.

What is John McLaughlin's sign-off line on "The McLaughlin Group" (synd., 1982–)?
"Bye-bye."

POLICE AND DETECTIVE SHOWS

♦ ♦ ♦

Was "Dragnet" (NBC, 1952–59, 1967–70) really based on real cases?

Yes. It may have been the original true crime drama, with all shows fashioned from cases found in Los Angeles police files. All scripts were reviewed by the police and the Los Angeles City Attorney's office. .

Who was Joe Friday's partner in "Dragnet" (NBC, 1952–59, 1967–70) when the series was revived in 1967?

Bill Gannon, played by Harry Morgan. Jack Webb played Sergeant Joe Friday. Friday's previous partners were played by Barton Yarborough, Barney Phillips, Herb Ellis, and Ben Alexander.

Who played Charlie Chan on TV?
On "The New Adventures of Charlie Chan," a syndicated program in the 1956–57 season, the sleuth was played by J. Carroll Naish, an Irishman from New York.

Where was "The Naked City"?
It was New York City, where the ABC police drama was set and shot from 1958 to 1963.

Who narrated "The Untouchables" (ABC, 1959–63)?
Walter Winchell (1897–1972), the veteran newsman who began his television career with "The Walter Winchell Show" (ABC, 1952–55).

In what precinct in New York did Officers Toody (Joe E. Ross) and Muldoon (Fred Gwynne) work on "Car 54, Where Are You?" (NBC, 1961–63)?
The 53rd Precinct, located in the Bronx, where the series was shot.

Who played "Honey West"?
Anne Francis played the female private detective during the 1965–66 season on ABC. Her pet ocelot was named Bruce.

Who produced "The F.B.I." (ABC, 1965–74)?
As the announcer never failed to remind us, the show was a "Quinn Martin Production."

Who played Jonathan Steed's original partner in "The Avengers" (ABC, 1966–69)?

157

In the original British series, Patrick Macnee's Steed played opposite Honor Blackman as Cathy Gale. Blackman later became known as James Bond's love interest, Pussy Galore, in *Goldfinger*. By the time the series was imported to America in 1966, Diana Rigg—as Emma Peel—had replaced Blackman.

Who was "The Girl from U.N.C.L.E." (NBC, 1966–67)?
April Dancer, played by Stefanie Powers, in this short-lived spoof of NBC's popular "The Man from U.N.C.L.E." (1964–68).

Who played Batgirl on TV's "Batman" (ABC, 1966–68)?
Yvonne Craig. She appeared only in the second and final season. Batgirl's real identity was Barbara Gordon, Police Commissioner Gordon's daughter.

Who composed the eminently hummable theme for TV's "Batman" (ABC, 1966–68)?
Neal Hefti. Danny Elfman wrote the score for the 1989 movie.

Who wrote the catchy theme song for "Mission: Impossible" (CBS, 1966–73)?
Lalo Schifrin, composer for Clint Eastwood movies like *Dirty Harry* (1971) and *Magnum Force* (1973).

At the opening of "Mission: Impossible" (CBS, 1966–73), how long would it take for the tape to self-destruct?

Five seconds.

What was the name of the force that responded to the call?
The I.M. Force.

What show was a spinoff of "The Rockford Files" (NBC, 1974–80)?

"Richie Brockelman, Private Eye" (NBC, 1978), starring Dennis Dugan in the title role.

Did Peter Falk, aka Lieutenant Columbo, ever appear on the series "Mrs. Columbo" (NBC, 1979)?

No. It was never completely clear that the title character, Kate Columbo (Kate Mulgrew) was even married to the rumpled policeman. Midway through the short-lived series, the character was renamed Kate Callahan and the title became "Kate Loves a Mystery."

Did Natalie Wood ever appear on husband Robert Wagner's TV mystery "Hart to Hart" (ABC, 1979–84)?

She had a walk-on in the 1979 pilot. She was billed in the closing credits as Natasha Gurdin, her real name.

What were the real names of the characters nicknamed "Tenspeed and Brown Shoe" (ABC, 1980)?

Tenspeed was con artist E. L. Turner (Ben Vereen) and Brown Shoe was Lionel Whitney (Jeff Goldblum). The two ran a Los Angeles detective agency.

In what city was "Hill Street Blues" (NBC, 1981–87) set?
The city was never named. Some exteriors in the opening credits were filmed in Chicago.

What kind of car did Michael Knight (David Hasselhoff) in "Knight Rider" (NBC, 1982–86) ride?
A Pontiac Trans-Am named KITT (voice by William Daniels).

What actors have played Mickey Spillane's detective Mike Hammer on TV?
Two: Darren McGavin, in "Mickey Spillane's Mike Hammer" (synd., 1957–59); and Stacy Keach in "Mickey Spillane's Mike Hammer" (CBS, 1984–87).

On "Murder She Wrote" (CBS, 1984–), what is Jessica Fletcher's (Angela Lansbury's) middle name?
Beatrice.

Who designed the visual style of "Miami Vice" (ABC, 1984–89)?
Much of the credit goes to art director Jeffrey Howard, who won an Emmy for his efforts in 1985.

What role did Jerry Lewis play on the TV series "Wiseguy" (CBS, 1987–90)?
In a set of five episodes, he played New York garment mogul Eli Sternberg.

Who photographed the black-and-white '40s episode, "The Dream Sequence Always Rings Twice," on "Moonlighting" (ABC, 1985–89)?
Gerald Finnerman, who had also been the cinematographer on "Star Trek" (NBC, 1966–69). Finnerman was nominated for an Emmy for the episode.

What was the airdate of the "Moonlighting" (ABC, 1985–89) episode in which Maddie (Cybill Shepherd) and David (Bruce Willis) finally had sex?
The episode was first broadcast on March 30, 1987, after two years of verbal foreplay.

PUBLIC AND
NON-NETWORK
TELEVISION

♦ ♦ ♦

Where do you go to sell a show for syndication?
The National Association of Television Program Executives (NATPE) trade convention, held in January. There producers and distributors sell game shows, reruns, etc., to station managers and program directors.

What was the first British "educational blockbuster" miniseries to be carried by PBS?
Kenneth Clark's "Civilisation," first broadcast on BBC2 in 1969. It was followed by Alistair Cooke's "America" (BBC, 1972) and Jacob Bronowski's "Ascent of Man" (BBC, 1974).

Is Alistair Cooke American or British?
He was born in Manchester, England, on November 20, 1908, but has been an American citizen since 1941. Cooke has hosted PBS's "Masterpiece Theatre" since its inception in 1971.

What PBS station produces Masterpiece Theatre (PBS, 1971–)?
WGBH in Boston.

> *What was the first series broadcast on "Masterpiece Theatre" (PBS, 1971–)?*
> "The First Churchills," in twelve episodes beginning on January 10, 1971.

Who was the original Lord Peter Wimsey on PBS?
Ian Carmichael. Edward Petherbridge has also played the role. The "Lord Peter Wimsey" stories originally aired on the BBC in Great Britain (1972–75, 1987–) and have been carried by PBS on "Masterpiece Theatre" (1971–) and "Mystery!" (1981–).

Who were the parents of the family on "An American Family" (PBS, 1973)?
William (Bill) Loud and Pat Loud. Their five children included Lance, their twenty-year-old son. They lived in Santa Barbara, California. The twelve-hour series first aired in February 1973.

When did the PBS science series "Nova" premiere?
It has been on the air since 1974.

When did "Monty Python's Flying Circus" originally air?
The forty-five episodes originally ran on BBC television in Great Britain from 1969 to 1974.

> *Who did the animation on "Monty Python's Flying Circus"?*
> Terry Gilliam, the only American in the troupe. Gilliam has gone on to direct movies like *Brazil* (1985) and *The Adventures of Baron Munchausen* (1989).

> *Who were the other Pythons?*
> John Cleese, Graham Chapman, Eric Idle, Michael Palin, and Terry Jones.

At what address were the stairs in "Upstairs, Downstairs" (PBS, 1974–79)?
At 165 Eaton Place in London. The house actually filmed was No. 65, but to avoid lawsuits, the producers glued a "1" in front of the "65."

Who played the first four Roman emperors in TV's "I, Claudius" (BBC, 1976)?
Brian Blessed played Augustus, George Baker played Tiberius, John Hurt played Caligula, and Derek Jacobi played Claudius.

What is the first name of "Rumpole of the Bailey" (Thames, 1978–88)? What is his wife's first name?

Horace Rumpole (Leo McKern) is married to Hilda Rumpole (Peggy Thorpe-Bates, Marion Mathie). He usually refers to her as "She Who Must Be Obeyed." The series has appeared on PBS's "Mystery!" (1981–).

How long have Siskel and Ebert had a syndicated television show?

On their syndicated show, Gene Siskel and Roger Ebert have been putting thumbs up and down to movies since September 1982. They first gained national fame on PBS's "Sneak Previews" in 1977.

When was CNN established?

It began broadcasting in 1980.

Who were the original hosts of the cable news show "Crossfire" (CNN, 1982–)?

Liberal Tom Braden and conservative Pat Buchanan. In 1989, Braden was replaced by Michael Kinsley. During Buchanan's 1992 presidential campaign, several people filled in for him, including Robert Novak and Linda Chavez.

In cable TV language, what is a dedicated channel?

It is a channel that offers only one kind of programming—weather, rock music, home shopping.

How many cable networks does Ted Turner own?

He owns Cable News Network (CNN), Turner Broadcasting System (TBS), Turner Network Television

(TNT), and CNN Headline News. As of 1989, they accounted for 31 percent of basic cable viewing.

SCIENCE FICTION AND FANTASY

♦ ♦ ♦

What was the prop budget for "Captain Video" (Du-Mont, 1949–55)?
Twenty-five dollars per week, which covered items like Video Decoder Rings and Astra-Viewers.

On the TV show "Outer Limits" (ABC, 1963–65), whose voice used to intone, "There is nothing wrong with your television set; do not attempt to adjust the picture"?
Vic Perrin's.

What were the first names of the shipwrecked Robinsons in "Lost in Space" (CBS, 1965–68)?

Will Robinson (Billy Mumy) is easy to remember from the many scenes where the Robot shouts things like "Danger, Will Robinson!" The other Robinsons were his sisters Penny (Angela Cartwright) and Judy (Marta Kristin); his mother Maureen (June Lockhart); and his father John (Guy Williams). Also aboard the Jupiter II were Dr. Zachary Smith (Jonathan Harris) and Major Don West (Mark Goddard). Bob May played the Robot, with Dick Tufeld providing the voice.

What were the first names of Scott, Chekov, and Mc-Coy on "Star Trek" (NBC, 1966–69)?
Their first names are as follows:

> Montgomery Scott
> Pavel Andreivich Chekov
> Leonard McCoy

Who played Spock's love interest Leila on the "Star Trek" (NBC, 1966–69) episode called "This Side of Paradise"?
Jill Ireland.

What "Star Trek" episode features Spock with a beard?
"Mirror, Mirror," where Leonard Nimoy portrays an evil Spock in a barbaric parallel universe.

How long did the TV version of "Planet of the Apes" run on TV?

Four months, from September to December 1974 on CBS, six years after the successful movie first ran. Galen the chimpanzee was played by Roddy McDowall.

Who were the evil aliens in "Battlestar Galactica" (ABC, 1978–80)?
The Cylons. Patrick Macnee provided the voice of the Cylon leader.

What did the name "Max Headroom" (ABC, 1987) stand for?
Just before reporter Edison Carter (Matt Frewer) crashed a motorcycle, he saw the words, "Max Headroom, 2.3 m." His memory impulses create a new character—Max Headroom.

What is the name of the bar aboard the Enterprise on "Star Trek: The Next Generation" (synd., 1987–)?
Ten Forward. Whoopi Goldberg, as Guinan, runs it.

Who played the security officer who was killed off on "Star Trek: The Next Generation" (synd., 1987–)?
Denise Crosby was Lieutenant Tasha Yar.

SITUATION COMEDIES

♦ ♦ ♦

How many years was "The George Burns and Gracie Allen Show" (CBS) on radio before it started on TV?
Eighteen years—1932–1950.

> *How many years was it on both TV and radio?*
> One year—1950. The TV version ran until September 1958.

What was the first all-black sitcom?
"Amos 'n' Andy" (CBS, 1951–53) with Spencer Williams as Andy Brown and Alvin Childress as Amos Jones. Amos was a cabdriver, Andy a bachelor.

How many episodes of "I Love Lucy" (CBS, 1951–57) centered on Lucy's pregnancy and childbirth?

Eight shows. The first revealed that Lucy was pregnant; the eighth depicted her going to the hospital to have Little Ricky.

What was the name of the club where Ricky Ricardo (Desi Arnaz) played on "I Love Lucy" (CBS, 1951–57)?
In New York, he played at the Tropicana. When the family moved to Connecticut, he started his own club, the Ricky Ricardo Babaloo Club.

Who played Lucy Ricardo's (Lucille Ball's) mother on "I Love Lucy" (CBS, 1951–57)?
Mrs. McGillicuddy was played by Kathryn Card.

> *Who played Fred Mertz's (William Frawley's) father?*
> Charles Winninger appeared in that role in 1954.

What was Lucy's character's name on "I Love Lucy" (CBS, 1951–57)?
Lucy McGillicuddy Ricardo.

> *On "The Lucy Show" (CBS, 1962–68)?*
> Lucy Carmichael.

> *On "Here's Lucy" (CBS, 1974)?*
> Lucy Carter.

What was Miss Brooks's first name?

Connie. The character was played by Eve Arden on "Our Miss Brooks" from 1952 to 1956 on CBS.

How long was "The Adventures of Ozzie and Harriet" (ABC) on radio before it started on TV?
Eight years—1944–52.

> *How many years was it on both TV and radio?*
> Two years—1952–54. The TV version continued until September 1966.

What was the longest-running sitcom?
"The Adventures of Ozzie and Harriet," which ran for fourteen seasons (1952–66) on ABC.

What was Mr. Peepers's first name on "Mr. Peepers" and what did he teach (NBC, 1952–55)?
Robinson J. Peepers taught biology.

What did "Make Room for Daddy" (ABC, CBS, 1953–64) mean?
It meant the kids had to move out of the master bedroom when their show-business father (Danny Thomas) returned from a tour.

What was Sergeant Bilko's full name and to what branch of the service did he belong?
Ernie Bilko (Phil Silvers) served in the army in "The Phil Silvers Show," which ran from 1955 to 1959.

What was the question Ralph Kramden ("The Honeymooners," CBS, 1955–56) missed when he appeared on "The $99,000 Answer"?
Who is the composer of "Swanee River"?

What is the correct answer?
Stephen Foster. Ralph guessed Ed Norton.

On "The Honeymooners" (CBS, 1955–56), what are the requirements for membership in the Raccoon lodge?
The applicant must have obtained a public school diploma, must have resided in the United States for the past six months, and must pay a $1.50 initiation fee. Ed Norton (Art Carney) objects that because of the residency rule, Anthony Eden could not become a Raccoon.

How many cast members have received residuals from the endless reruns of "The Honeymooners" (CBS, 1955–56)?
Only Audrey Meadows, who played Alice Kramden. Her manager negotiated for TV residual rights before most people took them seriously.

From what show was "The Andy Griffith Show" (CBS, 1960–68) a spinoff?
"The Danny Thomas Show" (ABC, CBS, 1953–64).

Who played Beulah the maid in "Beulah" (ABC, 1950–53)?

Two people: Ethel Waters (1950–52) and Louise Beavers (1952–53).

Who played Hazel the maid in "Hazel" (NBC, CBS, 1961–66)?
Shirley Booth was Hazel Burke.

Who played Alice Nelson, the housekeeper in "The Brady Bunch" (ABC, 1969–70)?
Ann B. Davis.

Where did Rob and Laura Petrie of "The Dick Van Dyke Show" (CBS, 1961–66) live?
They had a house in New Rochelle, New York.

On "The Dick Van Dyke Show" (CBS, 1961–66), what did the alien that Rob (Dick Van Dyke) feared look like?
Danny Thomas. The aliens had eyes in the backs of their heads.

Who were Dickens and Fenster and what did they do for a living?
Harry Dickens (John Astin) and Arch Fenster (Marty Ingels) were carpenters and handymen. They starred in "I'm Dickens—He's Fenster" (ABC, 1962–63).

What was the real name of "Gidget" (ABC, 1965–66)?
Francine Lawrence, played by Sally Field.

What was the name of the housekeeper on "Family Affair" (CBS, 1966–71)?
Giles French (Sebastian Cabot).

> *On "The Courtship of Eddie's Father" (ABC, 1969–72)?*
> Mrs. Livingston (Miyoshi Umeki).

> *On "The Jetsons" (ABC, 1962–63)?*
> Rosie the Robot (voice by Jean VanderPyl).

Who were "He and She" (CBS, 1967–68)?
Real-life married couple Richard Benjamin and Paula Prentiss played Dick and Paula Hollister. He was a cartoonist, she a social worker. They lived in New York.

What spinoffs did "The Andy Griffith Show" (CBS, 1960–68) spawn?
"Mayberry, RFD" (CBS, 1968–71) and "Gomer Pyle, USMC" (CBS, 1964–70).

What did Gomer Pyle do before he joined the Marines?
He was the gas station attendant in Mayberry on "The Andy Griffith Show" (CBS, 1960–68).

What was the name of the high school in "Room 222" (ABC, 1969–74)?
Walt Whitman High School.

> *In "Welcome Back, Kotter" (ABC, 1975–79)?*

James Buchanan High School.

In "Head of the Class" (ABC, 1986–91)?
Millard Fillmore High School.

Who played the Partridges in TV's "The Partridge Family" (ABC, 1970–1974)?
Shirley Jones (Shirley); David Cassidy (Keith); Susan Dey (Laurie); Danny Bonaduce (Danny); Jeremy Gelbwaks (Christopher, 1970–1971); Brian Forster (Christopher, 1971–1974); and Suzanne Crough (Tracy).

What were the names of the Pigeon Sisters on "The Odd Couple" (ABC, 1970–75)?
Cecily and Gwendolyn Pigeon, played by Monica Evans and Carole Shelley, respectively.

Who played the boyfriend of Myrna the secretary (Penny Marshall) on "The Odd Couple" (ABC, 1970–75)?
Her one-time husband Rob Reiner. The boyfriend's name was Sheldn (not "Sheldon"; they forgot the "o" on his birth certificate).

Where did Archie and Edith Bunker of "All in the Family" (CBS, 1971–79) live?
704 Houser Street in Queens, New York.

How many spinoffs did "All in the Family" (CBS, 1971–79) have?

Four: "Maude" (CBS, 1972–78); "The Jeffersons" (CBS, 1975–85); "Archie Bunker's Place" (CBS, 1979–83); and "Gloria" (CBS, 1982–83).

What was the name of Hawkeye Pierce's (Alan Alda's) tent on "M*A*S*H" (CBS, 1972–83)?
The Swamp.

What was Hawkeye's real name on "M*A*S*H" (CBS, 1972–83)?
Benjamin Franklin Pierce.

How many spinoffs did "The Mary Tyler Moore Show" (CBS, 1970–77) have?
Three, all on CBS—"Rhoda" (1974–78); "Phyllis" (1975–77); and "Lou Grant" (1977–82).

When did the pilot for "Happy Days" (ABC, 1974–84) first appear?
In February 1972, as a segment of "Love, American Style" (ABC, 1969–74), called "Love and the Happy Days."

How many spinoffs did "Happy Days" (ABC, 1974–84) generate?
Three:

"Laverne and Shirley" (ABC, 1976–83)
"Mork and Mindy" (ABC, 1978–82)
"Joanie Loves Chachi" (ABC, 1982–83)

What was the name of the cab company on "Taxi" (ABC, 1978–83)?

The Sunshine Taxi Company, in New York City.

What was the governor's name on "Benson" (ABC, 1979–86)?

James Gatling (played by James Noble).

> *What was the governor's name on "The Governor and J.J." (CBS, 1969–72)?*
>
> William Drinkwater (played by Dan Dailey).

Where is the exterior of the bar in "Cheers" (NBC, 1982–) filmed?

At a Boston bar called "The Bull and Finch" on Beacon Street across from the Boston Common.

What were the professions of "The Golden Girls" (NBC, 1985–92)?

Dorothy (Beatrice Arthur) was a teacher; Rose (Betty White) was a counselor; Blanche (Rue McClanahan) was an art-gallery assistant.

GIMMICK COMEDIES
♦ ♦ ♦

Who were Arnold Ziffel's parents on "Green Acres" (CBS, 1965–71)?
His human parents were Fred and Doris Ziffel of Hooterville. His porcine parentage is unknown.

What were some of the "critters" Elly May (Donna Douglas) had on "The Beverly Hillbillies" (CBS, 1962–71)?
They included a bear, a pigeon, a rooster, a cat, a dog, a skunk, and a hippopotamus.

Who produced the CBS "rural sitcoms" of the 1960s—"The Beverly Hillbillies" (1962–71), "Petticoat Junction" (1963–70), and "Green Acres" (1965–71)?
Paul Henning.

What was McHale's first name on "McHale's Navy" (ABC, 1962–66)?
Quinton, as in "Lieutenant Commander Quinton McHale" (Ernest Borgnine).

> *What was Captain Binghamton's first name?*
> Wallace (Joe Flynn).

> *What was Ensign Parker's first name?*
> Charles (Tim Conway).

What was the stalag number on "Hogan's Heroes" (CBS, 1965–71)?
Stalag 13.

> *What was the PT boat number on "McHale's Navy" (ABC 1962–66)?*
> PT 73.

Who played the Kravitzes on "Bewitched" (ABC, 1964–1972)?
Veteran character actor George Tobias played Abner Kravitz. Alice Pearce was the original Gladys Kravitz; Sandra Gould replaced her when Pearce died in 1966.

On "Bewitched" (ABC, 1964–72), how did Samantha (Elizabeth Montgomery) work magic?
She wiggled her nose.

> *How did Jeannie on "I Dream of Jeannie" (NBC, 1965–70) do it?*

She folded her arms in front of her and blinked.

How did Uncle Martin on "My Favorite Martian"
(CBS, 1963–66) do it?
He pointed at objects to levitate them and raised his
antennae to become invisible.

Who wrote "The Ballad of Gilligan's Island"?
George Wyle and "Gilligan's Island" producer Sher-
wood Schwartz.

**What were the full names of the following "Gilligan's
Island" (CBS, 1964–67) characters?:**
They were . . .

Gilligan—Gilligan (Bob Denver)
The Skipper—Jonas Grumbly (Alan Hale, Jr.)
The Millionaire—Thurston Howell III (Jim Backus)
His Wife—Mrs. Lovey Howell III (Natalie Schaefer)
The Movie Star—Ginger Grant (Tina Louise)
The Professor—Roy Hinkley (Russell Johnson)
Mary Ann—Mary Ann Summers (Dawn Wells)

**What was Agent 99's (Barbara Feldon's) name on
"Get Smart" (NBC, CBS, 1965–70)?**
It was never revealed, although on one episode she had
the cover name of Susan Hilton.

**What kind of a car was the title character in "My
Mother the Car" (NBC, 1965–66)?**

A 1928 Porter with Ann Sothern's voice. The "Porter" is a fictitious make.

Who were the lead cave dwellers befriending the lost astronauts on "It's About Time" (CBS, 1966–67)?
Joe E. Ross was Gronk and Imogene Coca was Shad.

Whose hand played Thing on "The Addams Family" (ABC, 1964–66)?
Ted Cassidy's. He also played the butler, Lurch.

What was the Flying Nun's name ("The Flying Nun," ABC, 1967–70)?
Sister Bertrille, born Elsie Ethington (played by Sally Field).

> *What was the name of her convent?*
> Convent San Tanco, in Puerto Rico.

On what novel was "The Flying Nun" (ABC, 1967–70) based?
The Fifteenth Pelican by Tere Rios.

Who played the married butler and cook for millionaire David Wayne in "The Good Life" (NBC, 1971–72)?
Larry Hagman and Donna Mills, future stars of "Dallas" (CBS, 1978–91) and "Knots Landing" (CBS, 1979–).

What was the chimp's name on "Me and the Chimp" (CBS, 1972)?

Buttons, played by Jackie. The chimp's human sidekick was Mike Reynolds, played by Ted Bessell.

What was the name of the "Love Boat" (ABC, 1977–86)?
It was the *Pacific Princess,* with Captain Merrill Stubing (Gavin MacLeod) at the helm.

Where did Alf, Uncle Martin, and Mork come from?
Their home planets are as follows:

Alf (voice by Paul Fusco)—Melmac
Uncle Martin (Ray Walston)—Mars
Mork (Robin Williams)—Ork

Who played Mork and Mindy's baby on "Mork & Mindy" (ABC, 1978–82)?
Jonathan Winters, who hatched from an egg sprouted from Mork's navel in 1981.

SOAP OPERAS AND GAME SHOWS

What was the longest-running prime-time game show?

"What's My Line?" It ran seventeen years from 1950 to 1967 on CBS.

What is the longest-running daytime TV drama?

"Search for Tomorrow" (CBS, 1951–1982; NBC 1982–1987). However, "The Guiding Light" is the longest daytime drama to run on both radio and TV. It began its run on radio in 1937. It has been on CBS-TV from 1952 to the present.

What is the longest-running performance in daytime drama history?

Mary Stuart as Joanne Barron and Larry Haines as Stu Bergman, both on "Search for Tomorrow" (CBS, 1951–82; NBC, 1982–1987).

What was the first Mark Goodson-Bill Todman TV game show production?
"Winner Take All" (CBS, 1948–51, NBC, 1952). Other Goodson-Todman hits have included "Beat the Clock," "I've Got a Secret," "To Tell the Truth," "Password," "The Match Game," and "What's My Line."

Who won the most money on "The $64,000 Question" (CBS, 1955–58)?
It was eleven-year-old Robert Strom, who won $192,000.

Did "The $64,000 Question" (CBS, 1955–58) cost more than $64,000 to produce each week?
It cost only a small fraction of that, about $15,000 per weekly episode. This was much cheaper than another top-rated half-hour show of the period, "The Jack Benny Show" (CBS, NBC, 1950–65), which cost $42,000 an episode.

Who were the panelists on "What's My Line" (CBS, 1950–67)?
The seventeen-year Goodson-Todman production was hosted by John Daly and featured these panelists: Hal Block (1950–53), Arlene Francis, Dorothy Kilgallen (1950–65), Louis Untermeyer (1950–51), Bennett Cerf (1951–67), Steve Allen (1953–54), and Fred Allen (1954–56).

In what towns are the following soap operas set:
The towns . . .

"All My Children" (ABC, 1970–)—Pine Valley
"Ryan's Hope" (ABC, 1975–89)—New York City
"The Guiding Light" (CBS, 1952–)—Five Points
"The Edge of Night" (CBS, ABC, 1956–84)—
    Monticello (a violent midwestern city)
"The Secret Storm" (CBS, 1954–74)—Woodbridge,
    New York
"As the World Turns" (CBS, 1956–)—Oakdale, Ohio

What game show did Walter Cronkite host?
"It's News to Me" (CBS, 1951–54).

How long did "Queen for a Day" run on television?
From 1955–59 on NBC and from 1959–64 on ABC.

Who was the original host of "To Tell the Truth" (CBS, 1956–67)?
Bud Collyer was the host when the show ran on prime time on CBS. When it went into syndication in 1969, Garry Moore took over.

How long did the "G.E. College Bowl" run and who hosted it?
It ran from 1959 to 1970 on CBS and NBC, and was hosted until 1963 by Allen Ludden and after that by Robert Earle.

How long did the original "Jeopardy" run?
From 1964 to 1975. It was hosted by Art Fleming.

What did Monty Hall do before he hosted "Let's Make a Deal" (NBC, CBS, 1963–76)?

He was a medical school student in Manitoba, Canada.

On the original "Hollywood Squares" (NBC, 1966–80), who usually sat in the center square?

Acerbic comedian Paul Lynde. He also played Uncle Arthur on "Bewitched" (ABC, 1964–72). Lynde died in 1982.

On what TV game show does Carol Merrill's daughter appear?

Her daughter Hillary Saffire became the hostess on the new "Truth or Consequences" (syndicated) in 1987. Merrill herself was the hostess on "Let's Make a Deal" (NBC, 1963–68; ABC, 1968–76).

Did Mike Wallace ever host a game show?

Yes, he hosted five of them: "Majority Rules" (1949–50); "Guess Again" (1951); "Who's the Boss?" (1954); "The Big Surprise" (1956–57); and "Who Pays?" (1959). He became a correspondent on "60 Minutes" (CBS, 1968–) in 1968.

What parts did Ryan O'Neal and Mia Farrow play on "Peyton Place" (ABC, 1964–69)?

Ryan O'Neal was Rodney Harrington; Mia Farrow was Allison Mackenzie.

On what daytime drama did New York mayor Edward Koch once appear as himself?

"All My Children" (ABC, 1970–)

In what daytime soap operas did the following movie stars once act:

The stars . . .

Tom Berenger—"One Life to Live" (ABC, 1968–), playing Tim Siegel

Ellen Burstyn—"The Doctors" (NBC, 1963–82), playing Dr. Kate Bartok

Robert DeNiro—"Search for Tomorrow" (CBS, NBC, 1951–87)

Dustin Hoffman—"Search for Tomorrow"

Raul Julia—"Love of Life" (CBS, 1951–80), playing Miguel Garcia

Bette Midler—"The Edge of Night" (CBS, ABC, 1956–84)

Susan Sarandon—"A World Apart" (ABC, 1970–71), playing Patrice Kahlman; "Search for Tomorrow," playing Sarah Fairbanks

Kathleen Turner—"The Doctors," playing Nola Dancer

Christopher Walken—"The Guiding Light" (CBS, 1952–), playing Mike Bauer

Sigourney Weaver—"Somerset" (NBC, 1970–76), playing Avis Ryan

How long has Susan Lucci played villainous Erica Kane on "All My Children" (ABC, 1970–)?
Since the show's debut in 1970.

What TV game show announcer was famous for shouting "Come on down" on "The Price Is Right" (NBC, 1956–65; CBS, 1972–)?

Johnny Olson. Olson worked on the show from 1972 until his death in 1985.

What was the first American game show hosted by Alex Trebek?
"The Wizard of Odds" (NBC, 1973–74). The Canadian-born Trebek is now host of "Jeopardy!" (syndicated, 1984–).

What dollar amount was named in the original title of the "Pyramid" game shows?
The show that debuted on CBS in 1973 was "The $10,000 Pyramid." The ante has subsequently been upped to $20,000, $25,000, $50,000, and $100,000. The show has also appeared on ABC and in syndication.

On what daytime drama did the rock group the B-52s once perform?
"The Guiding Light" (CBS, 1952–)

How long has "Wheel of Fortune" been on the air?
The syndicated program with Pat Sajak and Vanna White has been on since September, 1983.

TV ACTORS

♦ ♦ ♦

Was Jay Silverheels (Tonto on "The Lone Ranger," ABC, 1949–57) an Indian?

Yes, a Mohawk who grew up on a reservation in Canada.

How did Jack Klugman get his start on TV?

He had small parts on Ed Norton's favorite series, "Captain Video," (DuMont, 1949–55).

What comedian was "The Toastmaster General of the U.S."?

George Jessel. His TV show, "The George Jessel Show," ran during the 1953–54 season on ABC.

Who was known as "Lonesome George"?

George Gobel. His TV series, "The George Gobel Show," ran from 1954 to 1960 on NBC.

What was Liberace's real name?
Wladziu Valentino Liberace.

How long has Jerry Lewis been chairman of the Muscular Dystrophy Drive?
Since 1950.

Before "The Tonight Show," did Johnny Carson and Ed McMahon work together?
Yes, on a game show called "Do You Trust Your Wife?" (CBS, 1956–57). On the show, Edgar Bergen was the host, Johnny Carson was the emcee, and Ed McMahon was the announcer.

Who played Danny Thomas's Uncle Tonoose on "Make Room for Daddy" (ABC, CBS, 1953–64)?
Hans Conried.

What was Danny Thomas's real name?
Amos Muzyad Jacobs (or Jahoob).

Who was the youngest actor to play the lead in his own TV series?
Jay North of "Dennis the Menace" (CBS, 1959–63) and Jon Provost of "Lassie" (CBS, 1957–64), tied at age seven. ("Lassie" actually ran from 1954–71, but Provost was not on all those years.)

What was the song that made Carol Burnett famous?
It was "I Made a Fool of Myself Over John Foster Dulles," which she introduced in a New York nightclub

in the late 1950s and debuted nationally on "The Tonight Show" with Jack Parr.

When did George Reeves shoot himself?
On June 16, 1959. The police ruled that the former star of "The Adventures of Superman" (1952–57) had committed suicide, though some have suspected murder. He was planning to be married at the time.

What was the name of Sally Rogers's (Rose Marie's) off-and-on boyfriend on "The Dick Van Dyke Show" (CBS, 1961–66)?
He was Herman Glimscher, played by Bill Idelson. After appearing on "The Dick Van Dyke Show," Idelson became a comedy writer. He also produced many of the episodes of "The Bob Newhart Show" (CBS, 1972–78) in its first year.

What were the names of Kate Bradley's (Bea Benaderet's) daughters on "Petticoat Junction" (CBS, 1963–70)? Where did they live?
The three daughters were named Billie Jo, Bobbie Jo, and Betty Jo. Billie Jo was played by Jeannine Riley (1963–65), Gunilla Hutton (1965–66), and Meredith MacRae (1966–70). Bobbie Jo was played by Pat Woodell (1963–65) and Lori Saunders (1965–70). Betty Jo was played by Linda Kaye (Henning) (1963–70). They lived at the Shady Rest Hotel in Hooterville.

Why did Dick York leave "Bewitched" (ABC, 1964–72)?

Primarily for health reasons. As a result of a back injury during the filming of *They Came to Cordura* (1959), he developed a degenerative spine condition. He has also said that he wanted to spend more time with his children and that "the atmosphere on the set of 'Bewitched' was extremely unpleasant." Dick Sargent took over the role of Darrin Stephens.

On what TV series was William Shatner a regular before "Star Trek" (NBC, 1966–69)?
"For the People" (CBS, 1965). Shatner played Assistant District Attorney David Koster.

On what TV series did William Shatner and Leonard Nimoy work together before "Star Trek" (NBC, 1966–69)?
Shatner and Nimoy both appeared in a 1964 episode of "The Man from U.N.C.L.E." (NBC, 1964–68) called "The Project Strigas Affair."

Who played the following villains on "Batman" (1966–68):
The bad guys . . .

Penguin—Burgess Meredith
Catwoman—Julie Newmar, Eartha Kitt, and Lee Meri-
    wether
Joker—Cesar Romero
Riddler—Frank Gorshin and John Astin
King Tut—Victor Buono
Egghead—Vincent Price

The Archer—Van Johnson
Lola Lasagne—Ethel Merman
Lord Marmaduke Ffogg—Rudy Vallee
The Siren—Joan Collins
Chandel—Liberace
Louie the Lilac—Milton Berle

Who were the characters in the original "Mission: Impossible" (CBS, 1966–73) team?
Agent Briggs (Steven Hill), Cinnamon Carter (Barbara Bain), Barney Collier (Greg Morris), Willie Armitage (Peter Lupus), and Rollin Hand (Martin Landau). James Phelps (Peter Graves) joined the cast in 1968.

What other TV supporting roles did Ann B. Davis play besides housekeeper Alice Nelson on "The Brady Bunch" (ABC, 1969–74)?
She was Charmaine "Shultzy" Schultz, secretary to Bob Cummings's fashion photo reporter Bob Collings on "Love That Bob" (ABC, 1955–59) and Miss Wilson on "The John Forsythe Show" (NBC, 1965–66).

What is Redd Foxx's real name?
John Sanford—the same last name as that given Fred Sanford, his character on "Sanford and Son" (NBC, 1972–77).

Does Charo have a last name?
Her real name is Maria Rosario Pilar Martinez. Among her TV credits is the role of Aunt Charo in "Chico and the Man" (NBC, 1974–78).

Who used to play Father Guido Sarducci on "Saturday Night Live" (NBC, 1975–)?
Don Novello, who has since gone on to occasional roles in films such as *The Godfather Part III* (1990).

Who played Hymie the Robot on "Get Smart" (NBC, CBS, 1965–70)?
Dick Gautier. He later played Robin Hood on "When Things Were Rotten" (ABC, 1975).

What were the names of "Charlie's Angels" (ABC, 1976–81)?
Kate Jackson as Sabrina Duncan, Farrah Fawcett as Jill Munroe, Cheryl Ladd as Kris Munroe, Jaclyn Smith as Kelly Garrett, Shelley Hack as Tiffany Welles, and Tanya Roberts as Julie Rogers.

In what series did *Playboy* centerfold Barbi Benton star?
She was Maxx, part of a rock group called Sugar, on the 1977–78 ABC series, "Sugar Time!"

What series was Larry Hagman offered the same year he was offered "Dallas" (CBS, 1978–91)?
"The Waverly Wonders" (NBC, 1978), a sitcom about a high school basketball coach (starring Joe Namath). Hagman favored this series, which lasted one month; but his wife advised him to take "Dallas."

What is Mr. T's real name?

Lawrence Tero. He was born in Chicago in 1952 and appeared as Sgt. Bosco "B.A." Baracus on "The A-Team" from 1983 to 1987.

Who played the Log Lady on "Twin Peaks" (ABC, 1990–91)?
Catherine Coulson.

Of what town has Sonny Bono been mayor?
Palm Springs, California, since 1988.

TV MOVIES AND MINISERIES

♦ ♦ ♦

When did "The Homecoming," the original pilot for "The Waltons" (CBS, 1972–77), air?
The TV movie starring Patricia Neal and Richard Thomas aired on CBS in 1971.

On the 1971 CBS miniseries "The Six Wives of Henry VIII," who played the wives?
Catherine of Aragon—Annette Crosbie; Anne Boleyn—Dorothy Tutin; Jane Seymour—Anne Stallybrass; Anne of Cleves—Elvi Hale; Catherine Howard—Angela Pleasence; and Catherine Parr—Rosalie Crutchley. Henry VIII was played by Keith Mitchell.

Who wrote and directed the TV movie "The Autobiography of Miss Jane Pittman" (CBS, 1974)?

Tracy Keenan Wynn wrote the screenplay, based on Ernest J. Gaines's novel, and John Korty directed. The film, starring Cicely Tyson as a 110-year-old former slave, won nine Emmys, including Emmys for Tyson, Korty, and Wynn.

How many people watched the concluding installment of "Roots" (ABC, 1977)?
Almost 100 million—nearly half the population of the United States. The miniseries was broadcast on eight consecutive nights beginning January 23, 1977. It became the most-watched dramatic show in TV history.

What part did Maya Angelou play in "Roots" (ABC, 1977)?
Nyo Boto.

Who played Maya Angelou in the TV movie based on her memoir "I Know Why the Caged Bird Sings" (CBS, 1979)?
Constance Good.

Who played Bud Abbott and Lou Costello in the TV movie about the duo?
Harvey Korman played Bud and Buddy Hackett played Lou in "Bud and Lou" (1978).

Who played Elvis Presley in the TV movie "Elvis" (1979)?
Kurt Russell, with songs dubbed by Ronnie McDowell. The film was directed by John Carpenter.

Who played Elvis in the short-lived TV series "Elvis" (ABC, 1989–90)?
Michael St. Gerard.

Who wrote the teleplay for the CBS TV movie "Playing for Time" (1980)?
Playwright Arthur Miller. Vanessa Redgrave played Auschwitz prisoner Fania Fenelon.

Who played the title characters in the TV movie pilot "Cagney and Lacey"?
Loretta Swit played Chris Cagney and Tyne Daly was Mary Beth Lacey in the 1981 movie. In the series (CBS, 1982–88), Meg Foster played Cagney in the first few episodes; she was replaced by Sharon Gless. Daly continued as Lacey.

Who played Adam's parents in the TV movie "Adam" (1983)?
Daniel J. Travanti and JoBeth Williams played John and Reve Walsh, who became crusaders for missing children after their child Adam was kidnapped and murdered. A sequel, "Adam: His Song Continues" (1986) followed, with Travanti and Williams reprising their roles.

Who played the Roman emperors in the miniseries "A.D." (Anno Domini) (NBC, 1985)?
James Mason played Tiberius, John McEnery played Caligula, Richard Kiley played Claudius, and Anthony Andrews played Nero.

What did the title "Lonesome Dove" (CBS, 1989) mean?

It was the name of a town in south Texas. Retired Texas ranger Gus McCrae (Robert Duvall) ran a ranch near there.

VARIETY SHOWS

◆ ◆ ◆

For how long was "Ted Mack's Original Amateur Hour" on TV?
Twelve years, from 1948 to 1960 on the DuMont network, ABC, NBC, and CBS. During that time, Pat Boone and Gladys Knight made their national television debuts.

Who hosted "The Miss America Pageant" (1954–) before Bert Parks?
John Daly hosted it the first year; Parks took over until 1980. Several hosts followed, including Ron Ely and Gary Collins. It is now cohosted by Regis Philbin and Kathie Lee Gifford.

What were the names of the four Lennon Sisters?
Diane, Peggy, Kathy, and Janet. They were regulars on

"The Lawrence Welk Show" (ABC, 1955–71) from 1955 to 1968.

How long was Jack Parr host of "The Tonight Show" (NBC, 1957–)?

The host of the late-night show began his run on NBC July 29, 1957, and ended it March 30, 1962. He followed Steve Allen, who hosted the show from 1954 to 1957. The show was not live; it was taped earlier in the evening, as it is now.

What were the names of the pigeons played by Red Skelton on "The Red Skelton Show" (CBS, NBC, 1951–71)?

Gertrude and Murgatroyd.

When did Johnny Carson take over NBC's "Tonight Show" (NBC, 1954–)?

In 1962. He left the show in May 1992.

> *When did he introduce Carnac the Magnificent? Aunt Blabby? Art Fern?*
> In 1964, 1964, and 1971 respectively.

What was the name of the Italian mouse on "The Ed Sullivan Show" (CBS, 1948–71)?

Topo Gigio.

During what years was Goldie Hawn a regular on "Rowan & Martin's Laugh-In" (NBC, 1968–73)?

1968–70.

During what years was Lily Tomlin a regular on "Rowan & Martin's Laugh-In"?
During 1970–73.

Who were the original hosts of "Hee Haw" (CBS, synd., 1969–)?
Country singers Roy Clark and Buck Owens.

When was "The Smothers Brothers Comedy Hour" (CBS, 1967–69) canceled?
April 1969.

When were Tiny Tim and Miss Vicky married on "The Tonight Show"?
December 17, 1969.

Who were the Ding-a-Ling Sisters?
The four dancers came from the larger dancing group, the Golddiggers. They appeared on "The Dean Martin Show" (NBC, 1965–74) from 1970 to 1973.

On "The Flip Wilson Show" (NBC, 1970–74), what was the name of the boyfriend of the character Geraldine?
Killer.

What was the church affiliation of Flip Wilson's "Reverend Leroy"?
The What's Happening Now Church.

When were Jim Henson and the Muppets regulars on "Saturday Night Live" (NBC, 1975–)?
1975–76.

Which Jackson siblings appeared on the variety series "The Jacksons" (CBS, 1976–77)?
Jackie, Marlon, Tito, and Michael of the original Jackson Five, along with brother Randy and sisters Maureen (Rebie), La Toya, and Janet. Jermaine, the fifth member of The Jackson Five, did not appear. The Jackson Five provided voices for the cartoon series "The Jackson Five" (ABC, 1971–73).

How long did Richard Pryor's TV show last?
"The Richard Pryor Show" (NBC) saw five episodes, from September to October, 1977.

Who hosted "Fernwood 2-Night" (synd., 1977)?
Barth Gimble, played by Martin Mull. He was the twin brother of Garth Gimble, a character on "Mary Hartman, Mary Hartman" (synd., 1976–78).

What were the full names of "Pink Lady and Jeff"?
Mie Nemoto and Kei Masuda were the popular Japanese musical team Pink Lady, whose American variety show lasted only one year (1980) on NBC. Jeff Altman was their American sidekick.

PART·III

◆ MOVIES ◆
AND
TELEVISION

FIRSTS AND LASTS
♦ ♦ ♦

Who was the first film director?
W. K. L. Dickson (1860–1935), Thomas Edison's assistant. He directed Edison's first films in 1889.

What was the first movie to rely heavily on film editing?
The Life of an American Fireman (1903), by Edwin S. Porter (1869–1941). Porter was the first person to piece together strips of film containing different scenes in order to tell a story. Before Porter, most movies were shot in one take from one camera position.

When was *Hamlet* first put to film?
In 1907, in a silent film produced by George Melies.

Who was the first actress to play Queen Elizabeth I?

The great Sarah Bernhardt, in *Queen Elizabeth* (1912, France).

What was the first feature-length comedy?

Tillie's Punctured Romance (1914), directed by Mack Sennett.

Where did Walt Disney's animated cartoons first appear?

In Kansas City in 1919, when Disney started working for the Kansas City Film Ad Company, which produced short cartoon commercials to be shown in local theaters. By 1922, Disney had developed his own series of theatrical cartoons, "Laugh-O-Grams," which were parodies of fairy tales.

Who was the first on-screen Don Juan?

It was John Barrymore in the 1926 movie *Don Juan*, the first movie to synchronize sound effects into a sound track.

How did the practice of movie stars' placing their footprints in front of Grauman's Chinese Theatre begin?

It was first an accident, started when Sid Grauman put his footprints into unset concrete outside his own theater in 1927.

What was Alfred Hitchcock's first sound film?

Blackmail (1929). He actually filmed two versions, sound and silent. In the sound version, the German star

Ann Ondra's voice was supplied by English actress Joan Barry.

Who introduced the use of "subjective sound"—a voice-over showing what a character is thinking?
Director Rouben Mamoulian in *City Streets* (1931). While Sylvia Sidney lay alone in bed, she "remembered" what Gary Cooper had said to her earlier—and Gary Cooper's voice was heard on the soundtrack.

What was Bette Davis's film debut?
Bad Sister (1931).

What was Katharine Hepburn's film debut?
A Bill of Divorcement (1932).

What was Claude Rains's American debut?
The Invisible Man (1933). As the title character, Jack Griffin, Rains was never visible until the last shot, but his voice was heard throughout.

What was the first outdoor movie to be filmed in three-strip Technicolor™?
The Trail of the Lonesome Pine (1936), directed by Henry Hathaway. It starred Sylvia Sidney, Fred Mac-Murray, and Henry Fonda. It was set in backwoods Kentucky in the early 1900s.

On what film was Jean Harlow working when she died?
Saratoga (1937).

In what year did NBC begin regular television transmission to the American public?
In 1939.

What was Gene Kelly's film debut?
For Me and My Gal (1942).

What was Montgomery Clift's first movie?
Red River (1948), in which he played Matthew Garth, the child informally adopted by John Wayne's character, Tom Dunson.

What was the first TV series to star a black woman?
The first was "Beulah" (ABC, 1950–53), starring successively Ethel Waters, Hattie McDaniel, and Louise Beavers as Beulah, a black maid. "Julia" (NBC, 1968–71), starring Diahann Carroll as nurse Julia Baker, was the second.

What was the first film in 3-D?
Bwana Devil (1952).

What was the first film to feature rock music?
Blackboard Jungle (1955). Bill Haley's "Rock Around the Clock" played over the opening credits.

What was the first soap opera to change its format from fifteen minutes to thirty minutes each weekday?
"As the World Turns" (CBS, 1956–).

What was Clint Eastwood's first screen appearance?

It was as a lab assistant in *Revenge of the Creature* (1955). His second appearance was as "Jonesy" in *Francis in the Navy* (1955).

What was Cecil B. DeMille's last picture?
The Ten Commandments (1956).

Where did Elvis Presley make his TV debut?
Not on "The Ed Sullivan Show" (CBS, 1948–71), but on "The Jackie Gleason Show" (CBS, 1952–55, 1956–57, 1962–70). Elvis first appeared there in January 1956.

What was Humphrey Bogart's last film?
The Harder They Fall (1956), directed by Mark Robson. Bogart died of cancer in 1957.

When did Jim Henson and the Muppets make their national TV debut?
It was in 1957 on "The Tonight Show" (NBC, 1954–), hosted then by Steve Allen. Kermit (only one year old at the time) sang "I've Grown Accustomed to Your Face" to a monster who ate its own face and tried to eat Kermit's as well.

When did the RKO movie studio come to an end?
In 1958, when it was sold to Desilu.

What was Robert Duvall's film debut?
As Boo Radley in *To Kill a Mockingbird* (1962).

What film was Marilyn Monroe working on when she died?
Something's Got to Give (1962).

What were the last feature film appearances of:

Humphrey Bogart—*The Harder They Fall* (1956)
Gary Cooper—*The Naked Edge* (1961)
Buster Keaton—*A Funny Thing Happened on the Way to the Forum* (1967)
Errol Flynn—*Cuban Rebel Girls* (1969)
Maurice Chevalier—*Monkeys Go Home* (1956)

What was the first episode of "Star Trek" to be televised?
"The Man Trap," televised as a "sneak preview" on September 8, 1966. The episode dealt with a creature on planet M-113 who lives on salt sucked from humans.

What was the first movie to show full frontal female nudity?
Hugs and Kisses (1966, Sweden).

What were Spencer Tracy's last words on film?
"Well, Tillie, when the hell are we going to get some dinner?"—the last words of *Guess Who's Coming to Dinner* (1967).

What was Jack Nicholson's first job in the movies?
Office boy in MGM's cartoon department.

What was Gloria Swanson's last film?
Airport 1975 (1974).

What was Bernard Herrmann's final movie score?
The Oscar-winning last score was for *Taxi Driver* (1976).

What was Meryl Streep's theatrical film debut?
Julia (1977).

What was James Cagney's last movie?
Ragtime (1981).

What was Kevin Costner's debut in a major film?
A one-word part in *Frances* (1982).

What was Geena Davis's screen debut?
Tootsie (1982), where she played the dressing-room mate of Dustin Hoffman.

When did Lucy, Ricky, Ethel, and Fred of "I Love Lucy" (CBS, 1951–57) die?
Lucille Ball (Lucy) died on April 26, 1989, at age 77. Desi Arnaz (Ricky) died December 2, 1986, at age 69. Vivian Vance (Ethel) died on August 17, 1979, at age 72. William Frawley (Fred) died on March 3, 1966, at age 79.

What was Bette Davis's last film?
Wicked Stepmother (1989).

What was David Lean's last picture?

A Passage to India (1984). He was scheduled to start on an adaptation of Joseph Conrad's *Nostromo* when he died in 1991.

What was the top-rated TV program in 1950?
"Texaco Star Theater" (NBC, 1948–56)

What was the top-rated program in 1960?
"Gunsmoke" (CBS, 1955–75).

What was the top-rated program in 1970?
"Marcus Welby, M.D." (ABC, 1969–76).

What was the top-rated program in 1980?
"Dallas" (CBS, 1978–91).

What was the top-rated TV program in 1990?
"Roseanne" (ABC, 1988–).

OMNIBUS

♦ ♦ ♦

How many feet of film does one second of screen time take up?
Each second of screen time, projected at the normal sound speed of 24 frames per second, takes up 1.5 feet of 35-millimeter film. A two-hour movie uses 10,800 feet of film—or a little over two miles.

Where does the word "video" come from?
It is Latin for "I see."

Who was Garry Moore's sidekick on "The Garry Moore Show" (CBS, 1958–67)?
Durward Kirby.

Who was Andy Griffith's sidekick on "The Andy Griffith Show" (CBS, 1960–68)?
Don Knotts (as Barney Fife, 1960–65).

Who was Adam West's sidekick on "Batman" (ABC, 1966–68)?
Burt Ward (as Robin, or Dick Grayson).

What were the names of the Lumière brothers and what did they do for film?

Louis (1864–1948) and Auguste (1862–1954) Lumière developed the first motion picture projector (which also served as a camera), the Cinematographe, patented February 13, 1895. December 28, 1895, is widely considered the birthday of cinema. This was the first time the Lumière brothers showed their films to paying customers at the Grand Café in Paris. The program of short subjects included the arrival of a train, workers leaving their factory, and *L'Arroseur Arrosé*, a brief farce that was the world's first fiction film.

What was the world's first film studio?

The Black Maria, built in 1893 by Thomas Alva Edison, near his laboratories in West Orange, New Jersey. Films were shot there for Edison's peepshow-style kinetoscope viewer.

Who was known as "The Handsomest Man in the World"?

Silent film star Francis X. Bushman (1883–1966).

What were dish houses?

During the Depression, they were movie houses that offered dishes as inducement for attending.

Was the John Davidson who appears in old movie credits any relation to TV's John Davidson?
No. The earlier John Davidson (1886–1968) was a character actor who usually played dapper, sinister foreigners in silent and sound films. His movies included *The Green Cloak* (1915), *Romeo and Juliet* (1916), *Dinner at Eight* (1933), *A Tale of Two Cities* (1935), and *Dick Tracy vs. Crime, Inc.* (serial, 1941). The later Davidson (1941–) is best known for TV shows like "The Girl With Something Extra" (NBC, 1973–74) and "That's Incredible" (ABC, 1980–84). At one time he had planned to enter the ministry.

Was Mr. Memory (Wylie Watson) in *The Thirty-Nine Steps* (1935) based on a real person?
Yes. Director Alfred Hitchcock said the man with the phenomenal memory was based on a music hall performer known as Datas.

What were *The Thirty-Nine Steps* (1935)?
According to Mr. Memory, "The Thirty-Nine Steps is an organization of spies, collecting information on behalf of the foreign office of—" At this point, he was shot.

What movie character was portrayed in newspapers as "Cinderella Man"?
Longfellow Deeds (Gary Cooper) in *Mr. Deeds Goes to Town* (1936). The newspaper reporter writing about (and falling in love with) him was Babe Bennett (Jean Arthur).

What was the first sound film about the life of Christ?

The French *Golgotha* (1937), directed by Julien Du-vivier. It starred Robert Le Vigan as Jesus, and Jean Gabin as Pontius Pilate.

How many people were in the lifeboat in *Lifeboat* (1943)?
Nine. The actors playing them were Heather Angel, Mary Anderson, Tallulah Bankhead, William Bendix, Hume Cronyn, John Hodiak, Henry Hull, Canada Lee, and Walter Slezak.

Was there a Hollywood Canteen?
Yes, it was more than the title of a 1944 movie featuring Joan Crawford and Bette Davis. During World War II, it was a gathering place in Hollywood for servicemen and -women. It was founded by Bette Davis and John Garfield.

How many times did Charles Laughton play Captain Kidd?
Twice—in *Captain Kidd* (1945) and in *Abbott and Costello Meet Captain Kidd* (1952).

What is a *mise-en-scène?*
Meaning literally the "playing of a scene," it refers in film theory to the content of an individual frame. Orson Welles, F. W. Murnau, and Max Ophuls are all considered masters of the *mise-en-scène*—masters of composing a shot.

What is montage?

The assembling together of images in a film, usually in quick succession, often dissolving into one another. It can be used to convey action and the passage of time—newspaper headlines and theater marquees flying by as a dancer rises to stardom—or, as in the work of Sergei Eisenstein, to evoke emotional responses from the viewer by juxtaposing shots in a jarring way.

What was Little Sheba?

It was the name of Lola Delaney's (Shirley Booth's) dog in *Come Back, Little Sheba* (1952).

When did the first issue of *TV Guide* appear?

What is now the magazine with the largest national circulation first appeared on April 3, 1953. It had editions in ten cities and an initial circulation of 1,560,000.

What happened to the DuMont network?

The DuMont network started operating in 1944 with station WABD in New York (now WNYW). It had financing from Paramount Pictures but lacked a radio network such as the other networks had. (Owning a radio network made it easier to sign up TV station affiliates.) Further, complicated court rulings prevented DuMont from owning as many stations as its rivals. The network ceased operating in 1956.

Who adopted the word "cameo" as a cinematic term for walk-on parts for well-known people?

Producer Michael Todd, who filled *Around the World in 80 Days* (1956) with forty-four cameo stars.

In how many movies did Elvis die?

In one, his first, *Love Me Tender* (1956). It was also the only one in which Elvis did *not* receive top billing. Its original title was *The Reno Brothers*, but the title was changed when a song from the movie, "Love Me Tender," became a hit.

What stuntman somersaults out of Ben-Hur's chariot during the chariot race in *Ben-Hur* (1959)?

Yakima Canutt's oldest son Joe. The younger Canutt was doubling for Charlton Heston and was accidentally tossed out of the chariot when the vehicle hit some wreckage on the racecourse. The shot was so effective that it was left in the movie, with the screenplay changed to explain it. Yakima Canutt himself, as second-unit director, supervised the filming of the race.

Who played these famous doctors?

Dr. Pasteur in *The Story of Louis Pasteur* (1936)—Paul Muni

Dr. Ehrlich in *Dr. Ehrlich's Magic Bullet* (1940)—Edward G. Robinson

Dr. Newman, U.S. Navy, in *Captain Newman* (1963)—Gregory Peck

Dr. Strangelove in *Dr. Strangelove* (1963)—Peter Sellers

What TV theme songs have hit the Billboard Top 10?

"Dr. Kildare": "Three Stars Will Shine Tonight," sung by Richard Chamberlain (reached #10 in 1962)

"Dragnet": "Dragnet Theme," Ray Anthony Orchestra (reached #3 in 1953)

"The Greatest American Hero": "Believe It or Not," by Joey Scarbury (reached #2 in 1981)

"Happy Days": "Happy Days," by Pratt and McLain (reached #5 in 1976)

"Hawaii-Five O": "Hawaii Five-O," by the Ventures (reached #4 in 1969)

"Hill Street Blues": "Hill Street Blues," by Mike Post, featuring Larry Carlton on guitar (reached #10 in 1981)

"S.W.A.T.": "S.W.A.T.," by Rhythm Heritage (reached #1 In 1975)

"Welcome Back, Kotter": "Welcome Back, Kotter," by John Sebastian (reached #1 in 1976)

"The Rockford Files": "The Rockford Files," by Mike Post (reached #10 in 1975)

For which show did a TV network president accept an Emmy and say, "This is the best show I ever canceled"?

It was "He and She," which ran in 1967–68 on CBS and starred Richard Benjamin and Paula Prentiss. The network president was Mike Dann, of CBS.

What was the powerhouse Saturday night lineup that baby boomers remember watching on CBS in the 1973–74 season?

8:00—"All in the Family"; 8:30—"M*A*S*H"; 9:00—"The Mary Tyler Moore Show"; 9:30—"The Bob Newhart Show"; 10:00—"The Carol Burnett Show."

Why was the 1981 Oscar telecast delayed one day?
Because on March 30, the day of the telecast, President Ronald Reagan was shot by John Hinckley, Jr.

How many channels did the average television get in the 1950s? In the 1980s?
According to A. C. Nielsen, an average home in 1953 got 3.8 stations. With the advent of cable, 1983 saw televisions get an average of 10.3 stations. An average home in 1990 received 11.7 stations.

Who played Santa Claus in *Santa Claus* (1985)?
David Huddleston.

Where was the cornfield in *Field of Dreams* (1989) filmed?
Near Dyersville, Iowa.

How many of Bing Crosby's sons have killed themselves?
Two of the four. Lindsay Crosby shot himself in 1989; Dennis Crosby shot himself in 1991.

Which movie epic is longer—*Gone With the Wind* (1939), or *Heaven's Gate* (1980)?
Gone With the Wind, by one minute. It runs 220 minutes. *Heaven's Gate* was originally shown at 219 minutes, but was later cut to 149 minutes.

TV TO MOVIES/MOVIES TO TV

♦ ♦ ♦

What science-fiction serial did Leonard Nimoy appear in before "Star Trek" (NBC, 1966–69)?
Zombies of the Stratosphere (1952). Nimoy played Narab, a Martian.

What was the first movie based on a TV series?
It was *Dragnet* (1954), based on the NBC series of the same name (NBC, 1952–59, 1967–70).

In what Hitchcock film did Jerry Mathers (TV's Beaver on "Leave It to Beaver," CBS, ABC, 1957–63) appear?
The Trouble With Harry (1956). Mathers played Tony, Harry's son.

Who played Dolly Levi in the 1958 film version of the play *The Matchmaker*, on which *Hello, Dolly!* (1969) is based?

Shirley Booth took the part later played by Barbra Streisand. Booth won an Oscar for her performance in *Come Back, Little Sheba* (1952) and went on to become TV's "Hazel" (NBC, CBS, 1961–66).

What movie about a genie featured Barbara Eden?

The Brass Bottle (1964), starring Tony Randall. Eden played not the genie but Randall's girlfriend Sylvia. Burl Ives played Fakrash, the genie.

What was the name of Barbara Stanwyck's TV show?

She starred in two: "Barbara Stanwyck Theater" (NBC, 1960–61), a drama anthology that she hosted and in which she regularly performed; and "The Big Valley" (ABC, 1965–69), in which she played Victoria Barkley, matriarch of the Barkley clan.

Who played the Chief in *The Nude Bomb* (1980), the movie based on "Get Smart" (NBC, 1965–70)?

Not Edward Platt, who starred as the Chief in the series but who died in 1974. Dana Elcar, later the "chief" in "MacGyver" (ABC, 1986–), took the role.

> *What part did porn star Sylvia Kristel play in the film?*
> Kristel played Agent 34.

What movie was the basis for the TV show "Daktari" (CBS, 1966–69)?

Clarence the Cross-Eyed Lion (1965), with Betsy Drake and Marshall Thompson.

Did Richard Beymer and Russ Tamblyn ever team up between *West Side Story* (1961) and "Twin Peaks" (ABC, 1990–91)?

Yes, in *Free Grass* (1969). It also starred Natalie Wood's sister, Lana Wood.

What was "Radar" O'Reilly's real name in the 1970 film and 1972–83 CBS TV series "M*A*S*H*"?

Walter. Gary Burghoff played the character in both TV and film.

Was TV's "Bridget Loves Bernie" (CBS, 1972–73) based on a movie?

It was loosely based on *Abie's Irish Rose* (1946), in which an Irish girl named Rosemary (Joanne Dru) marries a Jewish boy named Abie (Richard Norris), leading to family conflict. In the TV show, Meredith Baxter played Bridget and David Birney played Bernie.

When did Elizabeth Taylor and Richard Burton appear on "Here's Lucy" (CBS, 1968–74)?

During 1973.

Did Jodie Foster ever star in a TV series?

Yes, during the 1974–75 season, she played Addie Pray on "Paper Moon," an ABC sitcom based on the 1972 Peter Bogdanovich movie.

What role did Corbin Bernsen of "L.A. Law" (NBC, 1986–) play in the black action film *Three the Hard Way* (1974)?

He played a "boy." The film, directed by Gordon Parks, Jr., starred Jim Brown, Fred Williamson, and Jim Kelly.

What part did Marlon Brando play in "Roots: The Next Generation" (ABC, 1977)?

American Nazi leader George Lincoln Rockwell.

What was Ron Howard's directorial debut?

Grand Theft Auto (1977). It featured Marion Ross, Howard's TV mom on "Happy Days" (ABC, 1974–84).

Who was first approached to play Indiana Jones in *Raiders of the Lost Ark* (1981)?

Tom Selleck, then known for his commercials for Chaz Cologne. He turned the offer down for the lead in a TV series—"Magnum, P.I." (CBS, 1980–88).

What part did John Ratzenberger (Cliff Clavin) of "Cheers" (NBC, 1982–) play in *Superman II* (1980)?

He was a staff person at NASA Mission Control in Houston.

226

What is the full name of Khan, the superhuman "Star Trek" villain?

Khan Noonian Singh (Ricardo Montalban). He was seen on the TV series (NBC, 1966–69) in an episode called "Space Seed" and in the theatrical movie *Star Trek II: The Wrath of Khan* (1982).

In what movie did "Family Ties" (NBC, 1982–89) star Michael J. Fox play a werewolf?

Teen Wolf (1985).

> *Who played the werewolf in the sequel,* Teen Wolf Too (*1987*)?
>
> Jason Bateman, star of "Valerie/The Hogan Family" (NBC, 1986–90; CBS, 1990–91).

Where did the Bedford Falls Company, producers of "thirtysomething" (ABC, 1987–1991), get its name?

From the town of Bedford Falls, New York, in *It's a Wonderful Life* (1947). The company's logo is a house in a snowstorm, based on the house in the movie, with the musical tag ". . . and dance by the light of the moon." That line comes from the song "Buffalo Girls, Won't You Come Out Tonight?" which is sung in the movie.

THE QUESTION AND
ANSWER HALL OF FAME

♦ ♦ ♦

Did James Cagney say "You dirty rat!" in any of his movies?
No.

What movie introduced the line, "If you want to call me that, smile"?
The Virginian (1929). Gary Cooper said it. Owen Wister, author of the novel *The Virginian,* phrased it as "When you call me that, smile!"

What were Greta Garbo's first spoken words on film?
"Gimme a whiskey, ginger ale on the side. And don't be stingy, baby." She said them in *Anna Christie* (1930).

How many films did Fred Astaire and Ginger Rogers star in together?
Ten. They are:
1. *Flying Down to Rio* (1933)
2. *The Gay Divorcee* (1934)
3. *Roberta* (1935)
4. *Top Hat* (1935)
5. *Follow the Fleet* (1936)
6. *Swing Time* (1936)
7. *Shall We Dance* (1937)
8. *Carefree* (1938)
9. *The Story of Vernon and Irene Castle* (1939)
10. *The Barkleys of Broadway* (1949)

What was the first movie to win all five top Oscars?
It Happened One Night (1934), from Harry Cohn's then "Poverty Row" studio, Columbia. In addition to winning the Oscar for Best Picture, the film brought honors to Frank Capra (director), Claudette Colbert (actress), Clark Gable (actor), and Robert Riskin (screenwriter).

To what does the *Variety* headline "Stix Nix Hix Pix" refer?
It refers to the idea that small-town residents do not like movies about small-town life.

What is the first spoken line in *Citizen Kane* (1941)?
"Rosebud," said by Charles Foster Kane (Orson Welles).

What is the last?

"Throw that junk in," said by Kane's butler, Raymond (Paul Stewart), as the "Rosebud" sled is thrown into the flames.

In what movie does the song "White Christmas" first appear?
Holiday Inn (1942), in which it is sung by Bing Crosby.

Did Dooley Wilson actually play the piano in *Casablanca* (1942)?
No. Wilson sang in the movie, but couldn't play piano. Accompaniment was dubbed in.

In what movie does Bette Davis say, "What a dump!"
Beyond the Forest (1949).

When did Lucy have her baby on "I Love Lucy" (CBS, 1951–57)?
January 19, 1953.

What was the name of the fraternal order to which Ralph Kramden and Ed Norton belonged ("The Honeymooners," 1956–57)?
The Raccoons.

> *What was the name of Ralph's bowling team?*
> The Hurricanes.

What was the name of the mysterious benefactor in "The Millionaire" (CBS, 1955–60)?

The man who gave away $1 million each week was named John Beresford Tipton. He was never seen; his voice was provided by Paul Frees, who also provided the voice of Boris Badenov on "The Bullwinkle Show" (ABC, NBC, 1959–63).

When was *The Wizard of Oz* (1939) first broadcast on TV?
November 3, 1956, from 9:00 to 11:00 P.M. EST on CBS. It got a 33.9 rating and a 52.7 percent audience share.

When were the TV quiz show scandals?
From 1958 to 1959.

Was it actually Anthony Perkins or a stand-in who stabbed Janet Leigh in *Psycho* (1960)?
It was a stand-in, a young woman wearing a wig.

What is Holly Golightly's (Audrey Hepburn's) real name in *Breakfast at Tiffany's* (1961)?
Lulumae Barnes, wife of Doc Golightly (Buddy Ebsen) from Tulip, Texas.

When did Jacqueline Kennedy lead a nationally televised tour of the White House?
In 1962.

What actor tells Dustin Hoffman in *The Graduate* (1967) the one word: "Plastics"?
Walter Brooke.

**What did Jack Nicholson finally order at the diner in
Five Easy Pieces (1970)?**
A plain omelet, a cup of coffee, and a chicken salad
sandwich on wheat toast—hold the butter, lettuce, may-
onnaise, and chicken (i.e., just bring the toast).

**Who provided the voice of Carlton the Doorman on
"Rhoda" (CBS, 1974–78)?**
Lorenzo Music. He was never seen.

**When did the first "All in the Family" (CBS, 1971–
79) air?**
January 12, 1971, at 9:30 P.M.

When did Edith Bunker die?
She died after "All in the Family" (CBS, 1971–79) had
become "Archie Bunker's Place" (CBS, 1979–83). The
1980–81 season opened with Archie grieving over her
death, which was not portrayed directly.

**What was Chuckles the Clown's sign-off line on "The
Mary Tyler Moore Show" (CBS, 1970–77)?**
"A little song, a little dance, a little seltzer down your
pants." The words were remembered by those mourning
Chuckles's death after he was killed by a rogue elephant.
Chuckles was dressed as Peter Peanut at the time.

When did Rhoda get married?
On October 28, 1974, Rhoda Morgenstern (Valerie
Harper) married Joe Gerard (David Groh). They sepa-

rated early in the 1976–77 season, and eventually divorced. "Rhoda" ran from 1974 to 1978 on CBS.

In his confrontation with a bank robber in *Dirty Harry* (1971), did Harry Callahan (Clint Eastwood) fire five shots or six?
Six. The robber was not shot.

Where in *The Godfather* (1972) does the line about "make him an offer he can't refuse" appear?
It appears three times:
- "My father made him an offer he couldn't refuse." Michael (Al Pacino) tells Kay (Diane Keaton) about Vito's (Marlon Brando's) threats against a bandleader.
- "I'm gonna make him an offer he can't refuse." Vito tells Johnny Fontane not to worry about movie producer Jack Woltz.
- "I'm gonna make him an offer he can't refuse." Michael tells Fredo (John Cazale) how he's going to buy out Moe Greene.

> *Does the phrase "an offer he can't refuse" appear in* The Godfather, Part II (*1974*)?
> Only once, in a variant form. Young Vito Corleone (Robert DeNiro) tells Clemenza (Bruno Kirby), with reference to Fanucci (Gaston Moschin), "I'll make him an offer he don't refuse."

Who shot J. R.?
Kristin Shepard (Mary Crosby), J. R.'s sister-in-law, in the last episode of the 1979–80 season of "Dallas"

(CBS, 1978–91). J. R. Ewing was played by Larry Hagman.

In what movie did Clint Eastwood say, "Go ahead. Make my day"?
Sudden Impact (1983).

What is the correct pronunciation of Demi Moore's first name?
Duh-MEE.

TRICK QUESTIONS AND POPULAR DELUSIONS

◆ ◆ ◆

What was the first all-talking movie?

It was not *The Jazz Singer* (1927), which only featured sound in parts, but *The Lights of New York* (1928), a Warner Brothers gangster movie. The *New York Times* called it "seven reels of speech."

In what movie did Charles Boyer say, "Come with me to the Casbah"?

Not in any movie. Many people have supposed incorrectly that he said it in *Algiers* (1938), where he played the French ne'er-do-well Pepe Le Moko living in the Casbah. Boyer said his press agent made it up.

What male actors appear in *The Women* (1939)?

None. The all-female cast includes Norma Shearer, Joan Crawford, Rosalind Russell, and Paulette Goddard.

Who sang for Lauren Bacall in *To Have and Have Not* (1944)?

Lauren Bacall. Andy Williams was hired to dub her voice, but Bacall's voice was used after all.

In what movie did Humphrey Bogart say, "Tennis, anyone"?

He never said it in any movie or play—though *Bartlett's Familiar Quotations* has quoted him as saying it.

How many directing Oscars did Alfred Hitchcock win?

None.

What was the first watch tested for durability on television?

It was not a Timex. In 1955, a Bulova "Clipper" watch attached to a weighted ball survived the "Niagara Falls Test."

Was *Lawrence of Arabia* (1962) Peter O'Toole's first film?

No. O'Toole played several secondary roles in *Ombre Bianche*, *Les Dents du Diable*, *The Savage Innocents*, *The Day They Robbed the Bank of England*, and *Kidnapped* (all 1960). He did not become famous until he appeared as T. E. Lawrence in *Lawrence of Arabia*.

How many female speaking roles are in *Lawrence of Arabia* (1962)?
None.

Who won the Cannes Film Festival prize for Best Film in 1968?
No one. Political demonstrations led by directors like François Truffaut, Jean-Luc Godard, and Claude Lelouch forced the festival to close in mid-proceedings that year.

Where does the sun set in the closing moments of *The Green Berets* (1968)?
In the east.

What British series was the basis for "All in the Family" (CBS, 1971–79)?
It is not "Till Death Do Us Part," but "Till Death Us Do Part" (BBC, 1966–68, 1972–74), starring Warren Mitchell as bigot Alf Garnett.

What movie preceded *Rambo III* (1988)?
Not *Rambo II*. There were three Rambo movies in the 1980s, all starring Sylvester Stallone as John Rambo, but none was called *Rambo II*. The three films were: First Blood (1982); Rambo: First Blood, Part II (1985); and Rambo III (1988).

Is Krakatoa east of Java?
No. The volcanic island of Krakatoa is in the Sunda Strait west of Java—making the title of the 1969 movie (*Krakatoa, East of Java*) incorrect.

BIBLIOGRAPHY

Allman, Kevin. *TV Turkeys: An Outrageous Look at the Most Preposterous Shows Ever on Television.* New York, NY: Perigee Books, 1987.

Anobile, Richard J., ed. *Michael Curtiz's Casablanca.* New York, NY: Darien House, 1974.

Anobile, Richard J., ed. *James Whale's Frankenstein.* New York, NY: Flare Books/Avon, 1974.

Armstrong, Richard B. *The Movie List Book: A Reference Guide to Film Themes.* Jefferson, NC: McFarland & Co., 1990.

Asherman, Allan. *The Star Trek Compendium.* New York, NY: Pocket Books, 1989.

Atwan, Robert, and Bruce Forer, eds. *Bedside Hollywood: Great Scenes from Movie Memoirs.* New York, NY: Moyer Bell Limited/Nimbus Books, 1985.

Biskind, Peter. *The Godfather Companion.* New York, NY: HarperPerennial, 1990.

Bogdanovich, Peter. *John Ford.* Berkeley, CA: University of California Press, 1978.

Bogle, Donald. *Blacks in American Films and Television.* New York, NY: Fireside, 1988.

Boller, Jr., Paul F., and John George. *They Never Said It: A Book of Fake Quotes, Misquotes, and Misleading Attributions.* New York, NY: Oxford University Press, 1989.

Boller, Jr., Paul F., and Ronald L. Davis. *Hollywood Anecdotes.* New York, NY: Ballantine Books, 1987.

Brooks, Tim, and Earle Marsh. *The Complete Directory to Prime Time Network TV Shows: 1946–Present.* New York, NY: Ballantine, 1985.

Brooks, Tim. *Complete Directory to Prime Time TV Stars: 1946–Present.* New York, NY: Ballantine Books, 1987.

Brosnan, John. *Movie Magic.* New York, NY: Plume, 1976.

Castleman, Harry, and Walter J. Podrazik. *Harry and Wally's Favorite TV Shows.* New York, NY: Prentice-Hall Press, 1989.

Chapman, Graham, et al. *The Complete Monty Python Flying Circus: All the Words, Vol. Two.* New York, NY: Pantheon, 1989.

Corey, Melinda, and George Ochoa. *The Man in Lincoln's Nose: Funny, Profound, and Quotable Quotes of Screenwriters, Movie Stars, and Moguls.* New York, NY: Fireside, 1990.

Crescenti, Peter, and Bob Columbe. *The Official Honeymooners Treasury.* New York, NY: Perigee, 1990.

Davis, Gerry. *The Today Show: An Anecdotal History.* New York, NY: William Morrow & Co., 1987.

Diamant, Lincoln. *Television's Classic Commercials: The Golden Years 1948–58.* New York, NY: Hastings House Publishers, 1971.

Eames, John Douglas. *The MGM Story.* New York, NY: Sundial, 1975.

Entertainment Weekly. New York, NY (various issues).

Fabe, Maxene. *TV Game Shows.* Garden City, NY: Dolphin/Doubleday & Co., Inc., 1979.

Floyd, Patty Lou. *Backstairs with Upstairs, Downstairs.* New York, NY: St. Martin's Press, 1988.

Gabler, Neal. *An Empire of Their Own: How the Jews Invented Hollywood.* New York, NY: Crown, 1988.

Garland, Brock. *War Movies.* New York, NY: Facts on File, 1987.

Gifford, Denis. *The British Film Catalogue, 1895–1985: A Reference Guide.* New York, NY: Facts on File, 1986.

Graham Jefferson. *COME ON DOWN!!! The TV Game Show Book.* New York, NY: Abbeville Press, 1988.

Greenfield, Jeff. *Television: The First 50 Years.* New York, NY: Crescent Books, 1977.

Halliwell, Leslie. *Halliwell's Filmgoer's and Video Viewer's Companion, 9th ed.* New York, NY: Harper & Row, 1988.

Halliwell, Leslie. *Halliwell's Film Guide, 7th ed.* New York, NY: Harper & Row, 1989.

Harmetz, Aljean. *The Making of the Wizard of Oz.* New York, NY: Alfred A. Knopf, 1981.

Harris, Jay S., ed., in association with the Editors of *TV Guide* magazine. *TV Guide: The First 25 Years.* New York, NY: Plume/New American Library, 1980.

Haun, Harry. *The Movie Quote Book.* New York, NY: Lippincott & Crowell, 1980.

Hibbin, Sally. *The New Official James Bond Book.* New York, NY: Crown Publishers, 1989.

Hirsch, Alan. *Talking Heads.* New York, NY: St. Martin's Press, 1991.

Howard, Sidney, Herb Bridges, and Terryl C. Brodman,

eds. *Gone With the Wind, The Screenplay.* New York, NY: Dell, 1989.

Hunter, Allan. *James Stewart.* Turnbridge Wells, Kent: Spellmount Ltd., 1985.

Information Please Almanac Atlas & Yearbook 1990, 43rd ed. Boston, MA: Houghton Mifflin Company, 1990.

Javna, John. *The Best of TV Sitcoms.* New York, NY: Harmony Books, 1988.

Kaatz, Ronald B. *Cable Advertiser's Handbook, 2nd ed.* Lincolnwood, IL: Crain Books, 1985.

Katz, Ephraim. *The Film Encyclopedia.* New York, NY: Perigee, 1979.

Lambert, Gavin. *GWTW: The Making of Gone With the Wind.* Boston, MA: Little, Brown & Co., 1973.

Langley, Andrew. *The Making of the Living Planet.* Boston, MA: Little, Brown & Co., 1986.

Lee, Spike, with Lisa Jones. *Do the Right Thing.* New York, NY: Fireside, 1989.

Maltin, Leonard. *Of Mice and Magic, rev. ed.* New York, NY: NAL, 1987.

Maltin, Leonard, ed. *Leonard Maltin's TV Movies and Video Guide, 1991 Edition.* New York, NY: Signet, 1990.

Marriott, John. *Batman: The Official Book of the Movie.* New York, NY: Bantam Books, 1989.

McCrohan, Donna. *The Honeymooners Companion.* New York, NY: Workman Publishing, 1978.

McGee, Mark Thomas. *Roger Corman: The Best of the Cheap Acts.* Jefferson, NC: McFarland & Co., 1988.

Michael, Paul, ed.-in-chief; James Robert Parish, associate ed.; and John Robert Cocchi; Ray Hagen; and Jack Edmund Nolan, contributing eds. *The American Movies.* New York, NY: Garland Books, 1969.

Monaco, James, and the editors of BASELINE. *The Encyclopedia of Film.* New York, NY: Perigee, 1991.

Mulay, James, J. *The Horror Film.* Evanston, IL: Cinebooks, Inc. 1989.

Nash, Jay Robert, and Stanley Ralph Ross. *The Motion Picture Guide.* Chicago, IL: Cinebooks, Inc., 1985.

New York Daily News. New York, NY (various issues).

New York Magazine. New York, NY (various issues).

New York Post. New York, NY (various issues).

The New York Times. New York, NY (various issues).

Norman, Barry. *The Story of Hollywood.* New York, NY: NAL, 1987.

Ogilvy, David. *Ogilvy on Advertising.* New York, NY: Vintage, 1985.

Parish, J. R. *The Great Science Fiction Pictures.* Metuchen, NJ: The Scarecrow Press, 1977.

Peary, Danny. *Cult Movies: The Classics, the Sleepers, the Weird, and the Wonderful.* New York, NY: Delta/Dell Publishing, 1981.

Peary, Gerald, ed. *Little Caesar.* Madison, WI: University of Wisconsin Press, 1981.

People. New York, NY (various issues).

Pickard, Roy. *Who Played Who in the Movies.* New York, NY: Schocken Books, 1981.

Premiere. New York, NY (various issues).

Quirk, Lawrence J. *The Films of Robert Taylor.* Secaucus, NJ: Citadel Press, 1975.

Radics, Bill, ed. *Theme from Mahogany and 12 Acad-*

emy Award Songs. Columbia Pictures Productions, 1977.

Rand McNally World Atlas 1970. Chicago, IL: Rand McNally, 1970.

Robertson, Patrick. *Movie Clips*. London, England: Guinness Books, 1989.

Robertson, Patrick. *Movie Facts and Feats*. New York, NY: Sterling, 1980.

Rosten, Leo. *Hollywood: The Movie Colony*. New York, NY: Arno Press, 1970.

Schemering, Christopher. *The Soap Opera Encyclopedia*. New York, NY: Ballantine Books, 1985.

Screen World Annuals. New York, NY (various years).

Shipman, David. *Movie Talk: Who Said What About Whom in the Movies*. New York, NY: St. Martin's Press, 1988.

Silver, Alain, ed.; Elizabeth Ward, ed.; and Carl Macek and Robert Porfirio, co-eds. *Film Noir, rev. ed.* Woodstock, NY: Overlook Press, 1988.

Steinberg, Cobbett. *Reel Facts: The Movie Book of Records*. New York, NY: Vintage Books, 1982.

Steinberg, Cobbett S. *Film Facts*. New York, NY: Facts on File, 1980.

Stetler, Susan L., ed. *Almanac of Famous People*. Detroit, MI: Gale Research Co., 1989.

Stine, Whitney. *I'd Love to Kiss You . . . Conversations with Bette Davis*. New York, NY: Pocket Books, 1990.

Thomas, Tony. *The West That Never Was*. Secaucus, NJ: Citadel, 1989.

Truffaut, François, with the collaboration of Helen G.

Scott. *Hitchcock*. New York, NY: Touchstone/Simon & Schuster, 1985.

Van Daalen, Nicholas. *The Complete Book of Movie Lists*. Toronto, Ontario: Pagurian Press, 1979.

Variety. New York, NY (various issues).

Vermilye, Jerry. *The Horror Films of the Twenties*. Secaucus, NJ: Citadel, 1985.

Waldron, Vince. *Classic Sitcoms: A Celebration of the Best in Prime-Time Comedy*. New York, NY: Macmillan Publishing Co., 1987.

Wiley, Mason, and Damien Bona, edited by Gail MacColl. *Inside Oscar*. New York, NY: Ballantine Books, 1988.

Winship, Michael. *Television*. New York, NY: Random House, 1988.

Woolery, George W. *Children's Television: The First Thirty-Five Years, 1946–81, Part I: Animated Cartoon Series*. Metuchen, NJ: The Scarecrow Press, 1983.

INDEX

♦ ♦ ♦

INDEX

INDEX

INDEX

INDEX

INDEX

INDEX

INDEX

INDEX

INDEX